Letts

GCSE Revision Notes

GCSE Science Higher

Authors
JOHN DOBSON
PAUL LEVY
NICK PARMAR

Series editor **ALAN BREWERTON**

Contents

Life processes and living things

Life processes and cell activity

Characteristics of living things	4	Cells, tissues, organs and systems	5
Cells	4		

Humans as organisms

Nutrition	7	Aerobic respiration	10
Digestion	7	Nervous system	10
Digestive system	7	Hormones	11
Circulation	8	Diseases	14
Respiration	9	Drugs	14

Green plants as organisms

Photosynthesis	16	Minerals and plant health	18
Photosynthesis and assimilation	17	Plant hormones	19
Transport of nutrients	18	Transport and water relations - transpiration	20

Variation, inheritance and evolution

Causes of variation	22	Genetic engineering	25
Cell division	22	Tissue culture	25
Human genetics	23	Cloning	25
Structure of DNA	24	Selective breeding	26
Protein synthesis	24	Evolution	26
Mutation	24	Natural selection	26

Living things and their environment

Adaptation and competition	28	Energy and nutrient transfer	30
Human impact on the environment	28	Use of microbes	31
Use of ecosystems	30	Carbon cycle	33
Artificial ecosystems	30	Nitrogen cycle	31

Materials and their properties

Classifying materials

Atomic structure	36	Bonding	37

Patterns of behaviour

Periodic table	41	Properties and uses of group	42
Group1 - alkali metals	41	8 (O) - noble gases	
Group 7 - halogens	41	Transition metals	42

Changing materials

Extracting iron from iron ore	44	Rusting	54
Electrolysis	45	Alcohols	55
Useful products from air	48	Solubility	57
Sulphuric acid: the Contact process	51	Water	58
		Chemical equations	60
Acids and alkalis	53	Rates of reactions	61
Indicators	54	Changes to the atmosphere	65

Physical processes

Electricity and magnetism

Electrostatics	70	Using electricity	71
Current electricity	70	Electromagnetism	72

Forces and motion

Representing motion	74	Momentum	76
Balanced forces	74	Circular motion	76
Friction	75	Pressure	76
Turning forces	75		

Waves

Properties of waves	78	Sound	81
Electromagnetic spectrum	79		

The Earth and beyond

The Solar System	84	Universe	85

Energy resources and energy transfer

Thermal energy	87	Energy resources	87
Energy efficiency	87	Work	88

Radioactivity

Atomic structure	90	Uses of radiation	91
Types of radiation	90	Half-life	91
Sources of radiation	90	Nuclear fission	91
Dangers of radiation	91		

Index   95

Life processes and cell activity

Characteristics of living things

Biology – science of living things.

- **Zoology** – study of animals.
- **Botany** – study of plants.
- **Microbiology** – study of bacteria, viruses, and fungi.

To be considered as living, all of the following seven characteristics must be present. Some non-living things have some of these characteristics but never all seven, e.g. a car can move, respire and feed (use oxygen to burn fuel) but it is not alive!

- **Movement** – living things can move – animals their whole bodies – plants parts of their bodies, e.g. leaves turn towards the Sun, flowers can open and close.
- **Respiration** – release of energy from food – essential to all life – provides energy to carry out living functions – most organisms use oxygen to respire.
- **Sensitivity** – living things detect and respond to changes in the environment – animals respond quickly by moving – plants usually respond slowly by growing.
- **Feeding** – all living things need food – provides energy through respiration and other essential substances, e.g. proteins, minerals etc.
- **Excretion** – removal from body of waste products, e.g. urea, carbon dioxide, water, from chemical reactions inside cells. Note: It is not removal of waste from digestion – this is called egestion or elimination.
- **Reproduction** – all living things produce young – plants and animals reproduce so that species continues after they die.
- **Growth** – all living things increase in size – animals grow until adult – some plants never stop growing.

> Remember these by the phrase MRS FERG: movement respiration sensitivity feeding excretion reproduction growth.

Cells

All living things are made up of cells.

Each living thing may be made up of millions of cells or just one cell, e.g. simple animal called Amoeba.

Animal cells

All animal cells have three basic parts:

- **cell membrane** – outside wall of cell – allows certain chemicals to move in and out of cell
- **cytoplasm** – contains many tiny structures which keep cell alive
- **nucleus** – control centre of cell – contains chemical information needed to make living thing.

Note: Human red blood cells do not have nuclei – more space to carry oxygen.

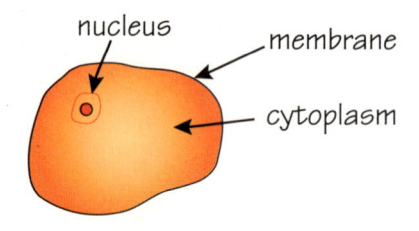

animal cell

> **Examiner's tip**
> It is very important to learn the names of the parts of plant and animal cells.

Plant cells contain all features of animal cells, but can have some extra ones.

Plant cells

- **Cellulose cell wall** – gives plant cell strength – makes it tough and rigid.
- **Vacuole** – a space filled with water – when full of water the plant cell is strong and rigid – said to be turgid.
- **Chloroplasts** – contains green chlorophyll – absorbs light which plant uses to make food to grow.

Test yourself! Can you draw and label the cell without looking at the diagram? This is important!

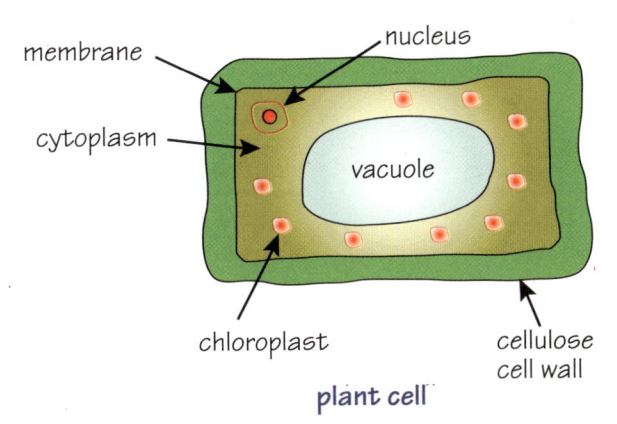

Plant cell diagram labels: membrane, nucleus, cytoplasm, vacuole, chloroplast, cellulose cell wall.

plant cell

Cells, tissues, organs and systems

Most living things have many different parts – e.g. animals have muscle, blood – plants have seeds, leaves.
The cells of these different parts have features that make them specialised to do certain jobs.

Cells can form:
- **tissues** – specialised groups of identical cells – have same job
- **organ** – many tissues grouped together – have same job
- **system** – a lot of organs grouped together – have same job
- **organism** – a lot of systems grouped together.

Examples

- **Muscle tissue** – contains lots of identical muscle cells.
  Lung – organ containing different tissues – muscle + blood + nerve + other tissues.
  Respiratory system – containing different organs – lung + trachea + diaphragm + ribs and muscles.
- **Glandular tissue** – a collection of glandular cells (producing enzymes etc.).
  Stomach – organ containing different tissues – glandular + nerve + muscle + blood + other tissues.
  Digestive system – includes different organs – mouth + oesophagus + stomach + intestines + other organs.
- **Xylem tissue** – lots of xylem cells (transport water in plants).
  Leaf – an organ which contains different tissues – xylem + phloem + mesophyll + epidermis.

Try to learn the names of some cells, organs and systems.

LIFE PROCESSES AND LIVING THINGS

LIFE PROCESSES AND LIVING THINGS

Questions

1. What is the study of plants called? _____
2. What is the study of animals called? _____
3. What is responding to changes in the environment called? _____
4. What is the release of energy from food called? _____
5. What is removing waste products from the body called? _____
6. What is removing the waste from digestion called? _____
7. What is producing new members of the species called? _____
8. What is increasing in size called? _____
9. Which gas is commonly used in respiration? _____
10. Which characteristic of living things is responsible for producing energy? _____
    _____
11. Name the seven characteristics of living things. _____
    _____
    _____
    _____
    _____
    _____
    _____
12. Which phrase helps you to remember these characteristics? _____
13. What are the inside contents of a cell called? _____
14. Which part of a cell controls its functions? _____
15. What is the outside of a plant cell called? _____
16. In which part of a plant cell is chlorophyll found? _____
17. Which part of a plant cell is filled with water? _____
18. What is a group of cells with the same function called? _____
19. What is a group of tissues with one function called? _____
20. What is a group of organs working for one function called? _____
21. What do a group of organ systems make up? _____
22. What features of plant cells do animal cells not have? _____
23. What is a neurone an example of? _____
24. What is the heart an example of? _____
25. What is the stomach an example of? _____

Humans as organisms

Nutrition

Humans need seven types of food in their diet:
- **carbohydrate** – e.g. starch, glucose, sugar, glycogen – used to make energy
- **protein** – made from amino acids – used for growth and repair of cells – enzymes and some hormones are proteins
- **fat** – made from fatty acids and glycerol – used to make energy – part of cell membranes
- **minerals** – like iron – red blood cells – lack of = anaemia, and calcium in bones and teeth – lack of = rickets.
- **vitamins** like C – lack of = scurvy, and lack of D in bones and teeth = rickets
- **water** – solvent for many chemicals in body
- **fibre** – roughage – helps food travel along digestive system.

Digestion

- Carbohydrate, protein and fat are insoluble.
- **Digestion** breaks down large, insoluble, complex molecules into smaller, simpler, soluble molecules.
- **Enzymes** carry out digestion – speed up chemical changes – catalysts.

Digestive system

Mouth

- Chewing begins to break up food – easier to swallow.
- **Saliva** lubricates food – easier to swallow.
- Saliva contains enzyme – carbohydrase – starts digestion of starch to glucose.

Oesophagus

- Gullet – food squeezed by muscular contractions – peristalsis – how food moves inside the gut.
- Produces no enzymes.

Stomach

- **Hydrochloric acid** kills germs and creates best conditions for enzymes.
- **Enzyme gastric protease** (pepsin) – digests protein to amino acids.

Duodenum

- **Bile** – made in the liver – stored in gall bladder.
- **Bile emulsifies fats** (breaks them into tiny droplets). Bile is not an enzyme – gives a large surface area for enzymes to work on.
- Bile also neutralises stomach acid.
- Digestive juice from pancreas – contains enzymes and neutralises acid from stomach – enzymes in duodenum need slightly alkaline conditions.
- **Lipase** – digests fat into fatty acids and glycerol.
- **Carbohydrase** – digests starch to glucose.
- **Proteases** – complete digestion of proteins to amino acids.

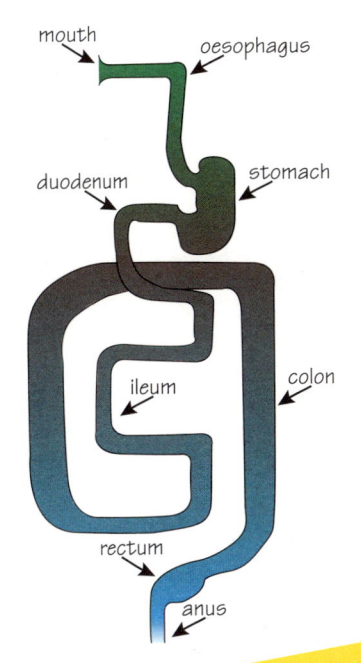

Copy the diagram and label it from memory.

LIFE PROCESSES AND LIVING THINGS

Ileum

- Enzymes complete digestion – **carbohydrase, protease** and **lipase** digest foods as above.
- Soluble, simple food absorbed into bloodstream.
- Adapted for diffusion of small molecules – large surface area – **villi**.
- Thin, moist, semi-permeable cell membranes – allow diffusion of food into blood.
- Active transport to absorb some food molecules – energy used by cells.

Note: **Duodenum** + **ileum** = **small intestine**.

> Remember the names of the organs of the digestive system with the word MOSDICRA
> Mouth Oesophagus Stomach Duodenum Ileum Colon Rectum Anus.

Large intestine - colon

- Water reabsorbed into blood – important as prevents dehydration.
- Indigestible food remains – **faeces**.

Rectum

- Stores faeces until they are eliminated through **anus**.

Circulation

Heart

Has four chambers:
- two **atria** at top
- two **ventricles** at bottom
- **right side** pumps blood to **lungs**
- **left side** pumps blood to **body**
- atria contract first – then ventricles.

Four valves:
- one between right atrium and ventricle
- one between left atrium and ventricle
- one at exit of right ventricle
- one at exit of left ventricle.

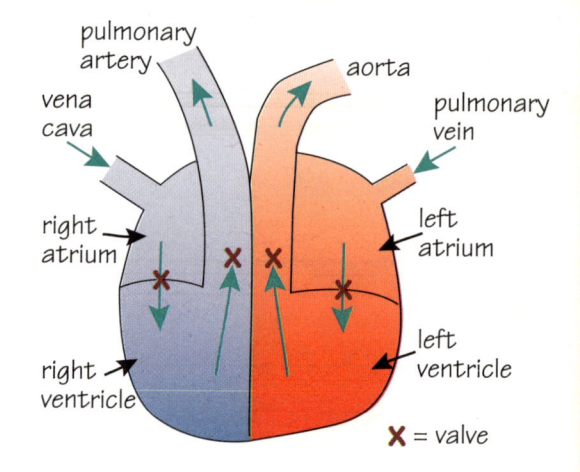

The valves stop blood flowing in wrong direction.

Heart – simple diagram

Blood flow

From major vein (vena cava) → right atrium → right ventricle → pulmonary artery → lungs (one circulation system) → pulmonary vein → left atrium → left ventricle → artery (aorta) → body (second circulation system).

Blood vessels

Arteries
- Thick walls – elastic – have muscle.
- Need to withstand high pressure.
- Carry blood **away** from the heart.
- Deep in the body for protection.

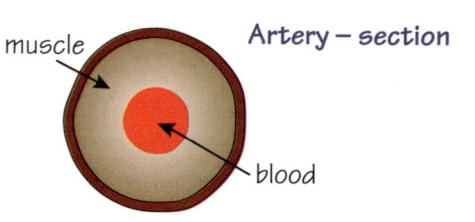

Veins
- Thinner walls than arteries.
- Have **valves** to keep blood flowing towards heart.
- Near muscles to help squeeze blood back to heart.

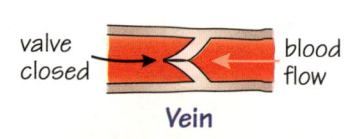

> Remember A = Artery = Away.

> Ve**in** = **into**

Artery – section

Vein

Capillaries
- Very thin – walls one cell thick.
- Exchange food, oxygen, carbon dioxide, waste, cell products, between blood and organs.
- Capillary exchange mechanisms in all organs, e.g. ileum, lung – alveoli, kidney – nephron.
- Provide very large surface area for diffusion.

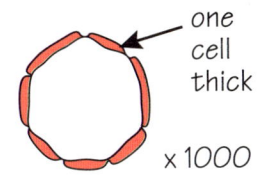

Blood

Contains **red cells**, **white cells**, **platelets** and **plasma**.

Red cells
- Carry **oxygen** in **haemoglobin**.
- Oxygen + haemoglobin → oxyhaemoglobin → in lungs.
- Oxyhaemoglobin → oxygen + haemoglobin – in capillaries near body cells – oxygen into cells for respiration.
- No nucleus – more room to carry oxygen.
- Made in bone marrow – live approximately 120 days.
- Poisoned by **carbon monoxide** – person suffocates from lack of oxygen.

White cells
- Have nuclei.
- Made in bone marrow.
- **Immunity** – defend the body against invaders – microbes, e.g. bacteria, viruses.
- Detect invaders and ingest (eat) them.
- **Antibodies** – made by white cells – destroy microbes and foreign tissue.
- **Antitoxins** – destroy poisons produced by microbes.
- **Immune system memory** – once you have had a disease you are immune – **vaccinations** trigger immune memory – **boosters** needed as a reminder for some diseases.

Note: You get lots of colds because the virus is different each time.

Platelets
- Made in bone marrow – from parts of much larger cells.
- React to cell damage/air.
- Produce fibres to trap red blood cells and **clot the blood**.

Plasma
- Liquid part of blood.
- Dissolves **carbon dioxide** – carries it to lungs.
- Carries dissolved **food from small intestine to liver** and all cells.
- Carries all cells.
- Carries **urea from liver to kidneys**.

Respiration

Lungs – special cells – ciliated epithelium – have cilia – clean lungs.

Breathing in
- Ribs move up and out – by muscles contracting.
- **Diaphragm** muscles contract – diaphragm moves down – flattens.
- Volume of chest increases.
- Pressure decreases (Boyle's law – physics).
- Air pressure forces air into lungs.

System includes: **trachea**, **bronchi**, **bronchioles**, **alveoli**.

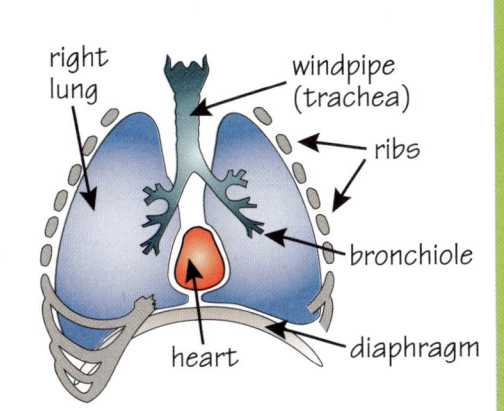

Alveoli
- Air sacs – provide a large surface area for gas exchange.
- Thin – about 2 cells between air in air sac and blood.
- Moist – lined with mucus – oxygen dissolves in mucus.
- Selectively permeable membranes – allow diffusion of gases.
- Good blood supply – capillaries cover alveoli – gases oxygen and carbon dioxide exchanged.

Internal respiration – production of energy within cells.

Aerobic respiration

> glucose + oxygen → carbon dioxide + water + energy

- Glucose carried in plasma.
- Oxygen carried in red blood cells.
- Cell cytoplasm – mitochondria – contains enzymes for respiration.
- Carbon dioxide carried away by plasma.
- Water – metabolic water – important source of water in desert animals.

Energy use
- Making molecules, e.g. proteins from amino acids.
- Muscle contraction.
- Heat production in birds and mammals – constant body temperature – homeostasis (see below).
- Active transport – diffusion of small molecules against a diffusion gradient, e.g. glucose in the kidney nephron, minerals in plant roots.

Exercise
- Muscles respire aerobically for a short time – they rapidly run out of oxygen – anaerobic respiration starts.
- Glucose broken into two molecules of lactic acid – energy released so muscles can continue to work.
- Lactic acid builds up as anaerobic respiration continues.
- Oxygen debt results – oxygen needed to remove all lactic acid after exercise.
- Anaerobic produces much less energy than aerobic.
- Carbon dioxide is not produced by anaerobic respiration.

Examiner's tip
Heavy exercise – still breathing – oxygen still entering muscles – aerobic respiration happens when enough oxygen present – carbon dioxide produced. Anaerobic respiration when not enough oxygen – lactic acid produced. Aerobic and anaerobic respiration can happen at same time.

Nervous system

Central nervous system (CNS)
- Brain.
- Spinal cord.

Neurons
- Sensory – messages from receptors to CNS.
- Motor – messages from CNS to effectors, i.e. muscles, glands and organs.
- Relay – mostly in CNS – messages between sensory and motor neurones.

Stimulus → receptor → co-ordinator → effector → response

Learn this.

Eye

- **Cornea** – transparent.
- **Sclera** – tough – protection.
- **Iris** – muscles control size of **pupil** – large in dim light – small in bright light.
- **Pupil** – hole for light to enter eye.
- **Retina** – light-sensitive cells.
- **Lens** – shape controlled by **suspensory ligaments** and **ciliary muscle**.
- **Optic nerve** – takes nerve impulses from retina to brain.
- **Fovea** – depression towards centre of retina where vision most acute.

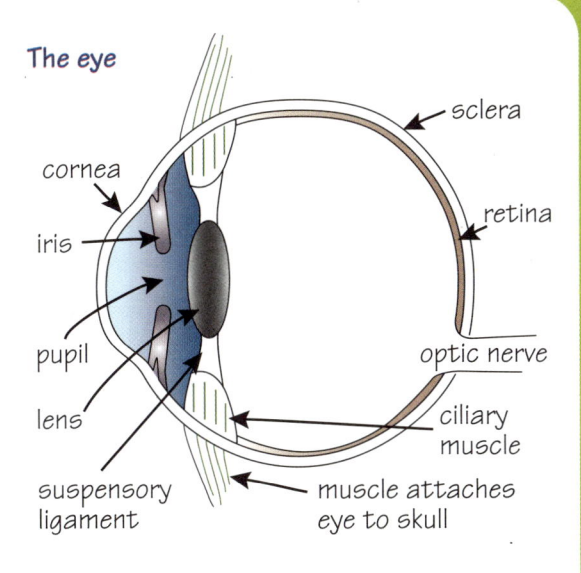

The eye

Image detection

Light enters eye → cornea and lens focus light on retina → receptor cells send message via optic nerve to brain → brain interprets image.

Focusing images

- Distant object – ciliary muscle relaxed – lens thin.
- Near object – ciliary muscle contracts – lens thick.

Reflex action, e.g. knee-jerk reflex

- **Receptor** detects **stimulus**, e.g. tap on knee.
- Sends message (**impulse**) – sensory nerve to **CNS** – **co-ordinator**, in this case = spinal cord.
- **Synapse** – gap between sensory neuron and relay neuron – chemical messenger crosses gap – **neurotransmitter** – passes impulse to relay neuron.
- **Synapse** – gap between relay and motor neuron – neurotransmitter – passes impulse to motor neuron.
- Motor neuron carries impulse to **effector**, in this case = thigh muscle.
- Effector produces **response**, in this case = leg moves forward.

Effectors make muscles move or glands secrete, e.g. saliva at the smell of food.

> **Examiner's tip**
>
> **Important** You must be able to analyse any given situation in terms of **stimulus → receptor → co-ordinator → effector → response**.

Hormones

Control and co-ordinate many body processes.

Blood sugar

Monitored and controlled by pancreas.

Glucose level in blood too high
- Pancreas releases **hormone insulin** into blood.
- **Insulin** picked up by **liver** from blood.
- Liver cells take glucose from blood – convert it to **glycogen** – stored.
- Blood sugar returns to normal.

Glucose level in blood too low
- **Pancreas** releases hormone **glucagon** into blood.
- **Glucagon** picked up by **liver** from blood.
- **Liver cells** convert **glycogen** to glucose – glucose released into blood.
- Blood sugar returns to normal.

Adrenaline 'flight or fight' hormone
- Produced by adrenal glands above kidneys.
- Prepares body for action.
- Increases respiration in muscle cells – more energy.
- Increase breathing rate – more oxygen.
- Increase release of glucose from liver – more food for cells.
- Dilate blood capillaries in limb muscles – more blood to cells.
- Muscles ready for action.
- Nervous system ready for action.
- Constrict blood vessels in gut – causes 'butterflies in stomach'.
- Resources in body diverted to where needed.

Menstrual cycle

Controlled by hormones from the **pituitary gland** in the brain and the **ovaries**.
- Day 1–5 – **period** occurs.
- Days 6–13 – **uterus** lining thickens caused by **oestrogen** and **progesterone** from ovary, prepares to receive fertilised ovum – ovum maturing, caused by hormone **FSH** from pituitary.
- Day 14 – ovulation – caused by hormone **LH** from pituitary.
- Day 15–28 – embryo implants. Or not pregnant – uterus lining stops developing – lack of hormones.
- Day 29 = day 1 – uterus lining shed if not pregnant – period.

Fertility treatment
FSH given – stimulates ovum development in ovaries – more than one may mature – multiple births.

Contraception
Oestrogen given – inhibits FSH production by pituitary – no eggs mature – none released.
Problem – body thinks it's pregnant – side effects – possible weight gain, sickness, long-term effects.
Take with medical supervision only.

Water balance

Hormone – **anti-diuretic hormone** – **ADH** – produced by **pituitary gland**. See **Homeostasis**.

Homeostasis

Control of the body's internal environment to keep it constant.

Lungs

- Remove carbon dioxide – waste product of respiration.
- Some water lost as breath is moist.

Liver
- Excess **amino acids** broken down into **urea** + carbohydrate.
- Carbohydrate – energy source – stored as **glycogen** or used in respiration.
- **Urea** enters blood and removed by **kidneys**.

Kidneys
- Filter the blood via kidney nephron.
- All small substances removed, e.g. water, urea, salt and glucose.
- Glucose needed by body – all glucose reabsorbed by nephron by **active transport** – cells use energy to do this.
- Some salt – sodium and chloride ions – reabsorbed.
- Water – see **Osmoregulation** below.
- Urea, salt ions and water are excreted – **urine** – stored in the **bladder** – eliminated as necessary.

Kidney failure
- Kidney machine used to keep patient alive – performs function of kidney.
- Dialysis three times a week.
- Transplant performed when one is available.
- Organ donor registry scheme – no longer need donor cards.

Osmoregulation – water regulation – most important job of kidney.
Brain monitors blood concentration.

Blood is too concentrated – not enough water
- Feeling of thirst – drink water.
- **Pituitary** produces **ADH** – travels in blood to kidney.
- Makes **kidney nephron more permeable** – reabsorbs water back into blood.
- **Urine is more concentrated** – less water lost.
- Blood returns to normal.

Learn this by drawing your own flow diagram!

Blood too dilute – too much water
- **Pituitary** releases less **ADH**.
- **Urine more dilute** – more water lost.
- **Kidney nephron is less permeable to water.**
- Blood returns to normal.

Skin
- Sweating – loses heat, water, salt ions and some urea; temperature control.

Temperature control
- Small animals cool faster than large animals – surface area/volume ratio. Thermoregulatory centre in brain monitors core body temperature.

Environment too hot
- Skin temperature **receptor** – causes impulse in sensory nerve → brain (co-ordinator).
- Brain sends messages – nerve impulse and hormone – to blood vessels in skin – dilate (get wider, vasodilation) – more blood to skin surface – more heat lost.
- Also message to sweat glands – sweat on skin – liquid evaporates – cool down.
  Note: capillary muscles = **effector**   dilating = **response**.

Environment too cold
- Brain and skin detect.
- Message to skin blood vessels to constrict (vasoconstriction) – less blood to skin – less heat lost.
- Brain – message to muscles to shiver – produces heat by respiration.

LIFE PROCESSES AND LIVING THINGS

Diseases

- Caused by **microbes** that invade body.
- Caused by **toxins** – poisons – produced by growing microbes.
- Growth of microbes in cells cause **cell death**.
- Made much worse by person being weak, e.g. in the disease AIDS.
- Usually need a lot of microbes to cause disease – unhygienic conditions, e.g. food poisoning (bacteria) – or contact with infection, e.g. chickenpox (virus).

Microbes

- **Bacteria** – much smaller than animal cells – contain cytoplasm, membrane and cell wall – genes in cytoplasm, not in a nucleus – most bacteria are harmless and very useful, e.g. grow in soil → nitrogen cycle – only a few cause disease.
- **Antibiotics** stop bacteria growing – penicillin stops cell wall production – bacteria burst and die.
- **Viruses** – much smaller than bacteria – contain protein and a few genes – can only grow inside living cells – take over cell functions – cell bursts open and dies when viruses reproduce.

Defence

- **Skin** – barrier to microbes.
- **Blood clot** – wounds quickly sealed – prevents entry of microbes.
- **Mucus** – sticky to trap microorganisms – protects nose, mouth, then lungs and stomach – open to outside.
- **Stomach** has acid – kills most microbes.
- **Immune system** – white blood cells – antibodies – see blood, circulation.

Drugs

These are any chemicals that enter the body and have an effect. They can be:
- **useful** – e.g. paracetamol – pain relief, antibiotics – kill microbes
- **harmful** – e.g. nicotine – dependence on cigarettes, alcohol – liver problems
- **very dangerous** – e.g. paracetamol – can be fatal with overdose, heroin – addictive, cocaine – addictive – withdrawal problems – very hard to quit.

Drug misuse

- Effect of drugs on a person depends upon person's state of health and mind.
- Same drug can affect two different people in very different ways.

Solvents

- Seriously affect behaviour, drug is in control.
- Damage to liver, lungs and brain.
- Most deaths caused by inhaling vomit when unconscious.

Tobacco

- Nicotine is addictive – affects blood pressure – calms people down – hard to give up.
- Other chemicals in cigarettes cause cancer – throat, lung, stomach, damage cilia.
- Breathing problems – emphysema, bronchitis.
- Carbon monoxide, in smoke – blood carries less oxygen – high blood pressure.
- Heart and blood vessels affected – heart disease, artery disease.

Alcohol

- Affects nervous system – small amounts – mild anaesthetic – slows reactions, larger amounts – affects motor control – movement, speech – person is not in control – coma – unconsciousness can follow – can be fatal.
- Heavy drinking for a long time causes severe liver damage – cirrhosis and sclerosis (hardening of tissue) – brain damage will result – death also.

Questions

1. Which three foods need digesting? _____
2. How does food travel along the digestive system? _____
3. What are the two functions of the acid in the stomach? _____
_____
4. What is the function of bile? _____
_____
5. What is the function of a protease? _____
6. Which chamber of the heart pumps blood to the lungs? _____
7. Which chamber of the heart pumps blood around the body? _____
8. Why do arteries have thick muscular walls? _____
_____
9. Why do veins have valves? _____
10. What is the function of red blood cells? _____
11. Name three things carried by blood plasma. _____
_____
12. Where in the lungs does diffusion take place? _____
13. Which type of respiration uses oxygen? _____
14. Which type of respiration does not use oxygen? _____
15. What is the order of events in any nervous response? _____
_____
16. Which organs make up the CNS? _____
17. Which hormone reduces blood sugar level? _____
18. Which hormone raises blood sugar level? _____
19. Which hormone causes ova to mature? _____
20. Which hormone causes ovulation? _____
21. What happens to excess amino acids in the body? _____
_____
22. What effect does ADH have on the kidney nephron? _____
23. What is the difference between bacteria and viruses? _____
_____
24. What causes people to be addicted to cigarettes? _____

LIFE PROCESSES AND LIVING THINGS

Green plants as organisms

Photosynthesis

- Plants **make food** by **photosynthesis**.

$$\text{carbon dioxide} + \text{water} \xrightarrow[\text{chlorophyll}]{\text{light}} \text{glucose} + \text{oxygen}$$

You must learn this equation.

- Photosynthesis controlled by **enzymes**.
- All **enzyme reaction rates are variable** depending on the conditions.

Carbon dioxide

- **Increased carbon dioxide** – **increased photosynthesis** – only up to the point where enzymes are working as fast as they can.
- Increase in carbon dioxide after this has little effect.
- Limited light will stop an increase in carbon dioxide from having any effect.

Examiner's tip
Look up the experiments on photosynthesis!
Remember:
you test leaves for starch using iodine, you need meths to remove the green colour from the leaf first!

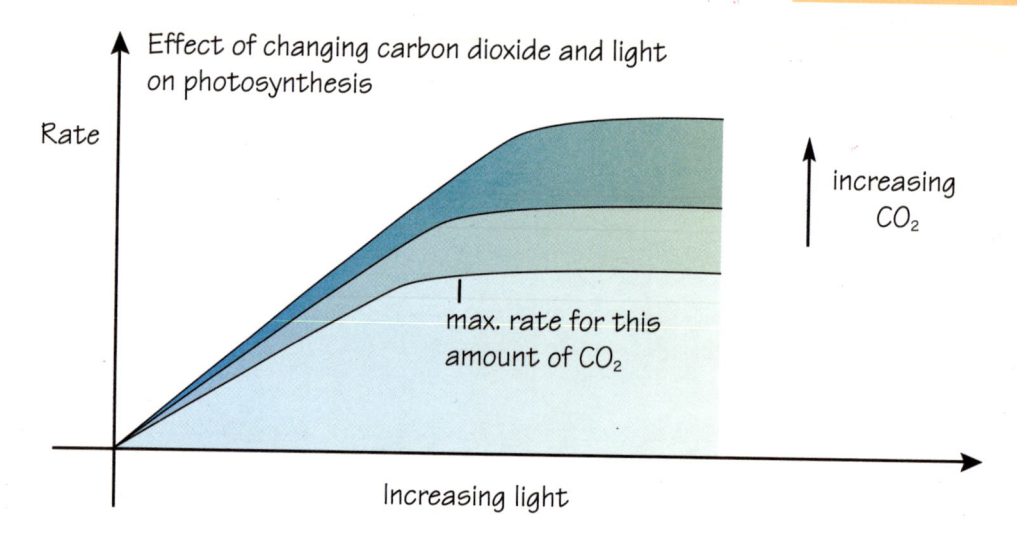

Effect of changing carbon dioxide and light on photosynthesis

Rate

max. rate for this amount of CO_2

increasing CO_2

Increasing light

Light

- **Increased light** – **increased photosynthesis** – until enzymes are working as fast as they can.
- Increasing light after this has little effect.
- Carbon dioxide limited – will stop increase in light from having any effect.
- Low temperature stops increase in light from having any effect.
- Light absorbed by **chlorophyll** in **chloroplast**.
- Not all plant cells have chloroplasts – e.g. **epidermal** cells have a different function – protect plant.
- Specialised cells in leaf called **palisade mesophyll** – specially adapted for photosynthesis – elongated shape to absorb light – more chloroplasts.

Temperature

- **Increased temperature** – rate of photosynthesis increases up to the optimum temperature for the enzyme.
- **Optimum temperature** – enzyme shape is a perfect fit (lock and key idea).
- Above this temperature enzyme shape starts to change – no longer fits perfectly – rate of reaction decreases – enzyme denatures at high temperature.
- Optimum temperature for photosynthesis different depending on environment plant is adapted to, e.g. desert plants adapted to higher temperatures than British plants.

> **Examiner's tip**
> When drawing graphs
> - **Use a pencil.**
> - Mark your points clearly with an X.
> - Draw a line of best fit.
> - Use as much of the graph paper as possible – use the largest scale you can.

Effect of changing temperature on photosynthesis

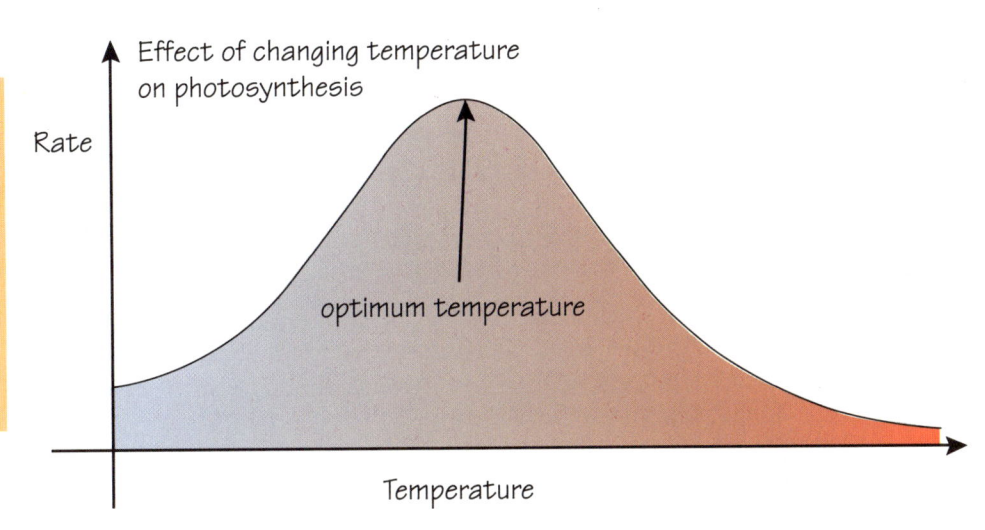

(Graph: Rate vs Temperature, bell curve peaking at optimum temperature)

Photosynthesis and assimilation

Assimilation means how food is used.

In plants the sugars produced by photosynthesis are:
- used to produce starch – stored as a future energy/raw material store
- converted to cellulose to make cell walls
- with addition of nitrogen and sometimes phosphorus and sulphur – converted into protein.

Also:
- **proteins** are used for growth
- **glucose** is used to produce energy needed for growth.

Plants store carbohydrate as starch and not sugars like glucose.
This is because:
- starch is insoluble
- glucose causes large amounts of water to enter cells by osmosis – starch does not
- osmosis – see later section.

Transport of nutrients

Glucose and other nutrients are transported by **phloem** cells – from leaves to:
- storage organs, e.g. roots
- growing regions, e.g. shoot tips.
* To make essential chemicals of life plants must absorb minerals through roots.
* Different minerals have different functions in plant.

Minerals and plant health

Nitrates

* **Essential** for the **synthesis of protein**.
* Remember **glucose** contains the elements carbon, hydrogen and oxygen.
* **Proteins** contain these together with **nitrogen**.
* Protein is needed to make **membranes**, **DNA**, **enzymes** and **chlorophyll**.

Nitrate deficiency

* Causes poor growth and yellowing of leaves.
* Little protein made – no new cells as no cell membranes made, no enzymes to control cells and no chlorophyll.
* Plants try to **compensate** – produce new leaves – have to move any nitrogen they have to the growth areas – older leaves become yellow and die off.

   Summary: **Plants** that are **stunted in growth** with **yellow older leaves** are **nitrate** or **nitrogen deficient**.

Potassium

* Needed for **synthesis** of **some enzymes**.
* Photosynthesis and respiration impaired – plant will have many problems.
* Cannot synthesise chemicals and produce energy.

Potassium deficiency

* Growth limited – not as badly affected as nitrate deficiency.
* Young leaves are yellow as **chlorophyll** synthesis restricted – enzyme problems.
* Leaves eventually turn green as plant moves resources to compensate – areas of cell death due to lack of enzymes.

   Summary: Potassium deficiency causes **yellow leaves with dead spots**.

Phosphate

* Needed to **synthesise some proteins** but not all.
* If essential proteins cannot be made growth will be affected.
* Phosphate has an **important role** in **photosynthesis** and **respiration**.

Phosphate deficiency

* Root growth severely affected – roots short with few side roots.
* Young leaves produced that are purple in colour.
* Chlorophyll not synthesised properly – enzyme problems.

   Summary: Phosphate deficiency causes **stunted root growth** and **purple younger leaves**.

Examiner's tip
Learn the three mineral summaries!

Plant hormones

- **Hormones** – control plant growth.
- **Shoots** grow towards light – phototropism – away from gravity – negative geotropism.
- **Roots** grow towards water and gravity – away from light.
- Shoots bend towards light because of hormone – auxin – causes lengthening of cells.
- Shoot tip produces auxin – this moves back down plant stem.
- Light deactivates auxin.
- If light from one side only – more auxin on shade side – this side lengthens more – shoot bends over towards the light.

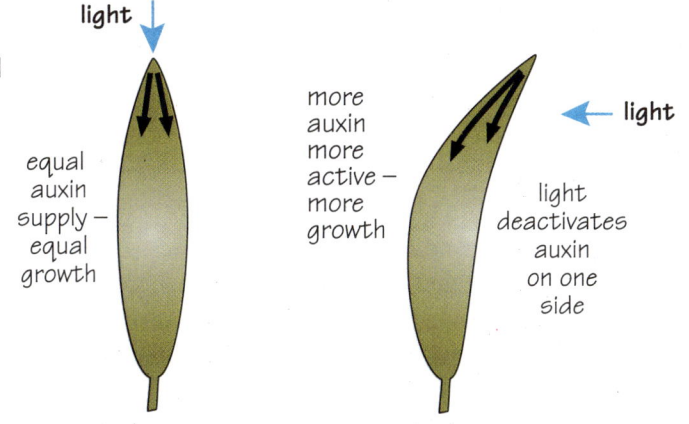

light ↓
equal auxin supply – equal growth

more auxin more active – more growth
← light
light deactivates auxin on one side

Roots

- Rooting powders – used to promote growth of stem cuttings.
- Hormone promotes the growth of healthy roots on the cut stem.
- Many plants produced very quickly by promoting root growth on many stem cuttings.

Fruit

- Hormones sprayed on flowers – causes formation of fruit – fruit has not been fertilised and is seedless.
- Fruit also bigger than normal – energy has not been used to produce seeds.
- Hormones also sprayed to speed up or slow down fruit development – on the tree or after fruit picked – farmer able to produce crop at best time for climate and market.

Weedkillers

- Growth hormones sprayed onto plants – grow too quickly – run short of energy and die.
- The hormones are selective for certain types of plant – weedkiller works from within – when the plant dies the hormone should be broken down in the soil.

Benefits

- Production of many new plants by cuttings – identical to the parent plant.
- Development of seedless fruit.
- Selective weedkillers that do not pollute the soil.

You may need to discuss this in the form of a short essay!

Problems

- What if the plant hormones aren't broken down in the soil? Can enter food chain – could cause problems for other plants and animals.

LIFE PROCESSES AND LIVING THINGS

Transport and water relations - transpiration

- Plants absorb most water through root hair cells – adapted to increase surface area for absorption.
- Plants lose water through leaves – dependent on the structure of the leaves.
- Water evaporates from spongy mesophyll cells → enters the spaces in leaf → diffuses towards the stomata pore → evaporates from the leaf.
- Water that is lost from the leaves is replaced by water from roots.
- Water flows from roots through stem and to leaves in xylem vessels.
- Movement of water called transpiration stream – fastest on hot, windy, dry, sunny days – slower on cold, wet and dark days.

Copy diagram and label cells from memory.

Water regulations

- Stomata – holes in underside of leaves – restrict the loss of water.
- Guard cells – special cells that open or close stomata.

Daylight/plant has a lot of water:
- photosynthesising as fast as possible
- stomata wide open to allow transpiration at maximum rate.

Plant is short of water/dark:
- stomata close – restricts water loss
- photosynthesis also slows down or stops.

Plants that live in dry climates are adapted to restrict water loss by:
- having thicker cuticle – prevents water evaporating from upper leaf surface
- reducing leaves to spikes, e.g. cacti.

Osmosis

Plant cells absorb or lose water by osmosis depending upon concentration of solutes.

- Gaining water – dilute outside cell – concentrated inside – water enters cell by osmosis – cell swells.
- Turgid – cell full of water – turgid cells important – gives cells support.
- Losing water – concentrated outside cell – more dilute inside – water leaves cell by osmosis – cell shrinks.
- Flaccid – when only a little water is lost – plant wilts.
- Plasmolysed – loss of too much water – plant dies.

Examiner's tip: Learn your teacher's definition of osmosis.

Example
Think of a plant cell as a football – the leather case is like cellulose cell wall – rubber inner tube is vacuole.
- The more air you blow into the football the harder it becomes – water entering the vacuole makes a plant cell turgid.
- If air is let out of the football it becomes soft – water leaving the plant vacuole makes the cell soft – plasmolysed.

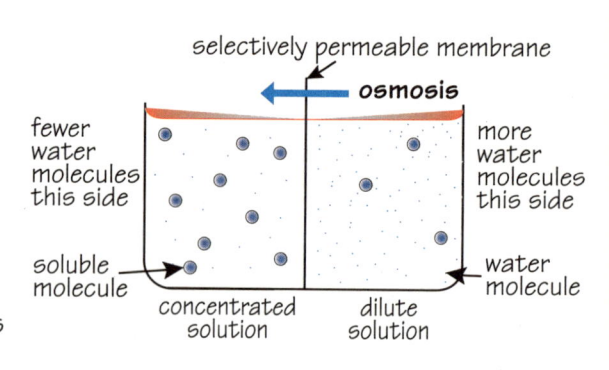

Questions

1. What is the green pigment in plants called and where in the cell is it found? _____

2. Which cells in the leaf are specially adapted for photosynthesis? _____ _____

3. What is the name of the cells in a plant that transport water? _____

4. What is the name of the cells that transport food in a plant? _____

5. What is the name of the cells in a plant that transport minerals? _____

6. In which conditions would photosynthesis be greatest? _____

7. In which conditions would photosynthesis be worst? _____

8. In which conditions would transpiration be very high? _____

9. In which conditions would transpiration be very low? _____

10. At which time of year is photosynthesis greatest? _____

11. What is the name of the process that describes how glucose leaves and enters a plant cell? _____

12. By what process does water leave and enter a cell? _____

13. What word describes a cell full of water? _____

14. What word describes a cell that is lacking in water? _____

15. Which mineral deficiency causes very poor growth in plants? _____

16. Which mineral deficiency causes young leaves to be purple in plants? _____

17. Which mineral deficiency causes any leaves to turn yellow? _____

18. Which mineral deficiency causes dead spots on leaves? _____

19. Which mineral deficiency causes stunted root growth? _____

20. Which mineral deficiency causes the plant's older leaves to turn yellow? _____

21. How do plant shoots respond to light? _____

22. How do plant roots respond to gravity? _____

23. How do plant shoots respond to gravity? _____

LIFE PROCESSES AND LIVING THINGS

Variation, inheritance and evolution

Causes of variation

Living things of the same species are different from each other owing to two factors:

- genes – different living things have different genes
- environmental – living things live in different environment – can affect how living things grow – not enough food or nutrients – animals and plants will not grow as well – too much competition in one place – animals or plants may be stunted in development – opposite could also be true if there was very little competition.

Genetics

- Studying how information is passed on from one generation to the next.
- Information is carried in genes which are found on chromosomes.
- Different genes control different characteristics.
- Different forms of same gene – alleles, e.g. brown and blue eye colour.
- Homozygous – individual has both alleles of a gene the same, e.g. XX, female.
- Heterozygous – individual has different alleles for a gene, e.g. XY, male.
- Dominant allele – characteristic always develops.
- Recessive allele – characteristic only develops when dominant allele not present.

You must learn the names used in genetics.

Chromosomes

- Genes are found on chromosomes.
- Chromosomes in pairs in all body cells of all animals and plants.
- In humans there are 46 chromosomes – 23 pairs in all body cells.
- Every cell has all genes that carry the information to make another copy of you.
- Chromosomes made from chemical called DNA.
- DNA has unique property that it can duplicate itself exactly.
- When cells divide they produce exact copies of chromosomes and genes.

Heredity

- Genes are passed on from one generation to next.
- Every living thing must reproduce to survive – passing genes to next generation.
- A living thing is a biological success if it leaves copies of its genes in its offspring.
- The more copies of its genes it leaves, the bigger a success it was.

Two forms of reproduction

- Sexual – this mixes genes – produces much more variation in living things – evolution can happen.
- Asexual – produces offspring that are identical – clones – all genetically same.

Cell division

Mitosis Body cell division – repair and growth.

- Cells divide – produce copies of themselves – all pairs of chromosomes duplicated exactly.
- Two new cell nuclei receive identical sets of paired chromosomes.
- All body cells have identical chromosomes – there are occasional mistakes – chromosome mutations.

Meiosis Production of sex cells

- Copies of chromosomes made in testes of males after puberty – in ovaries of females before they are born – in ovaries and anthers of plants.
- Pairs of chromosomes separated.
- Cell divides to form four sex cells – each cell only has one copy of the chromosome.

Human genetics

- Human cells have 46 chromosomes in nuclei.
- When ovum fertilised to produce baby, baby must also have 46 chromosomes.
- Sex cells – sperm and ova – have 23 chromosomes.
- Sperm and ovum contribute equally to embryo.
- 23 chromosomes from sperm + 23 chromosomes from ovum = 46-chromosome embryo.

Inheritance of sex

- Humans have sex chromosomes called X and Y.
- Females have two X chromosomes (XX).
- Males have one X and one Y (XY).
- When sex cells produced – sex chromosomes separate and end up in different cells.
- All ova have X chromosome only.
- Two types of sperm – one with Y chromosome – one with X chromosome.

```
mother XX      x        XY father
ovum    X               X or Y sperm

offspring XX            XY
          girl          boy
```

Cystic fibrosis

- Caused by **recessive gene** (c). N = normal dominant gene.
- Breathing and digestion problems – membranes do not secrete normally.
- Sufferers have a short life expectancy – treatment improving all the time.
- Adults can be normal but carry a recessive cystic gene – **carrier**.
- Condition usually runs in families but may miss generations.
- Parents Nc x Nc – 25% chance of a cystic child.

Huntington's chorea

- Caused by a **dominant gene**. (H) parent Hn x nn.
- Affects the nervous system – loss of motor and sensory function – quickly leads to death.
- Person will be perfectly normal until about 35 to 45 years of age – develop Huntington's chorea – become seriously ill and die.
- By this time may have had their family and passed the gene on to children.

Sickle cell anaemia

- Caused by **recessive gene**.
- Disease is inherited from both parents who carry the gene.
- Name comes from shape of the red blood cells that disease produces.
- **Sickle cell disease** is very serious.
- Gene is still in populations of people who live where there is **malaria** – carriers of the gene have a greater resistance to malaria than normal people.
- So in malaria areas – NN catch malaria and die – Ns survive – ss die of sickle cell anaemia (let N = normal and s = sickle cell).

- **Sex-linked conditions** – caused by Y chromosome in males having missing DNA.
- **Muscular dystrophy** – muscle wastage – fatal by adolescence.
- **Haemophilia** – cannot make factor 8 protein – clots the blood.
- Inherited from the mother – she carries a recessive gene on one of her X chromosomes.
- Father's X chromosome has a normal gene but Y chromosome has gene missing. E.g. haemophilia, **colour blindness.**
- Only males contract haemophilia.
- Haemophiliac males tend not to have children because of the difficulties caused by the disease.

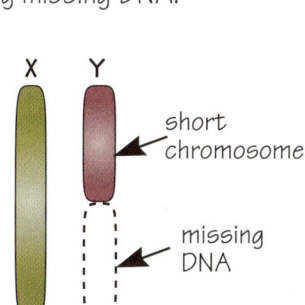

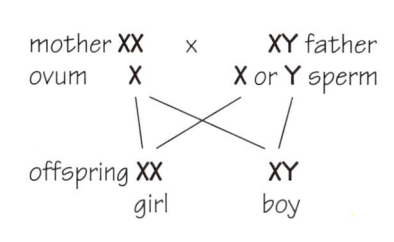

- Only males get one form of Muscular Dystrophy – it is passed on in the same way.
- Females can be colour blind even though it is inherited in the same way – colour blind males will want to have children as the condition is not life threatening.

Let C = normal vision and c = colour blind
Mother (XCXc) – a carrier   x   father (XcY–) – colour blind
There is a 25% chance of the genotype XcXc – a colour blind female.

Structure of DNA

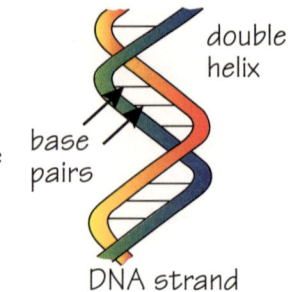

- Two long strands that coil around each other – form **double helix** shape.
- Strands linked together by **hydrogen bonds** – from one **base** to another.
- 4 bases (chemicals) in DNA – called A, T, C, and G.

DNA is able to replicate itself exactly.
- Double helix 'unzips' – each side acts as a template to build another DNA strand.
- Result is **two** double helixes of DNA.
- These separate into new cells as cell cytoplasm divides.
- Happens to **all** chromosomes (strands of DNA) at same time so the division of cells is co-ordinated.

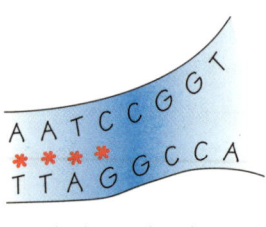

Examiner's tip
DNA structure and protein synthesis often confused in exams – be careful.

* = hydrogen bond

Protein synthesis

- Order of bases of DNA very important.
- Order codes for all proteins.
- Three nucleic acid bases code for one amino acid.

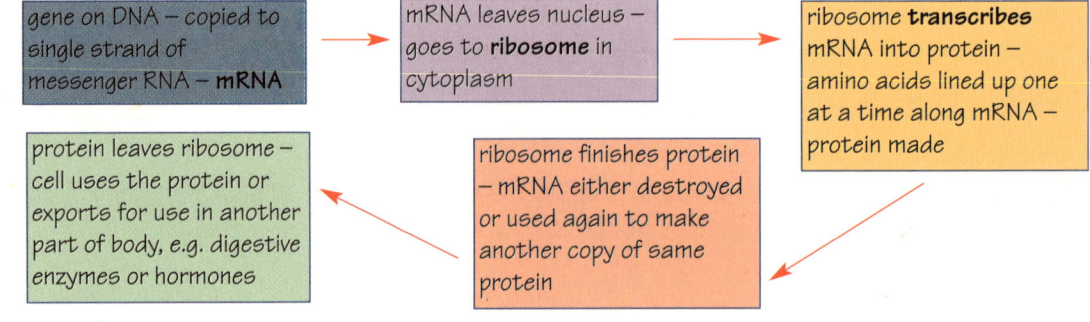

gene on DNA – copied to single strand of messenger RNA – **mRNA** → mRNA leaves nucleus – goes to **ribosome** in cytoplasm → ribosome **transcribes** mRNA into protein – amino acids lined up one at a time along mRNA – protein made → ribosome finishes protein – mRNA either destroyed or used again to make another copy of same protein → protein leaves ribosome – cell uses the protein or exports for use in another part of body, e.g. digestive enzymes or hormones

Mutation

- Change in gene code – DNA instructions changed.
- Gene mutations when ova and sperm being produced will be passed on to offspring – embryo will not survive if mutation too great – embryo usually non-viable.
- Only small mutations passed on this way, e.g. **Down's syndrome**.
- Down's syndrome – one sex cell (usually ovum) contains one extra chromosome – the embryo has 47 chromosomes instead of 46 in every cell – affects development – produces child with symptoms of Down's syndrome.

Chromosome changes in adults

- Cells divide and produce new cells – making new chromosomes can go wrong.
- **Mutations** can occur naturally with a mistake in replication of DNA.
- Dead cell is destroyed by immune system and no harm results.

- Some mutations caused by ionising radiation, e.g. ultra violet, gamma rays, X-rays.
- Also caused by chemicals such as tar from cigarettes.
- Greater exposure – more mutations – greater chance that cell survives – cell will replicate – pass mutation on to daughter cells.
- This mutation remains in the one organism unless it is where sex cells are made.
- Workers with radiation must be shielded and protected – e.g. lead jackets and shielded cubicles of radiographers, test badges of nuclear power workers.
- Cancer – cells lose ability to stop dividing – grow out of control.

Genetic engineering

When genes are artificially transferred from one living thing to another – between members of same or different species.

Plasmids

Pieces of bacterial DNA – can have other genes inserted, e.g. human factor 8, human insulin – plasmids carry new gene into bacterial cell – bacteria now makes human product – basis of genetic engineering – this is how human insulin is made.

Benefits

Conquering cystic fibrosis
- Healthy gene could be placed into cell in embryo.
- Replicates and provides the embryo with normal secretions in lungs.

Or
- Same gene could be transferred via virus directly into the lungs of cystic child.
- Virus genetically engineered to carry healthy gene – infects lungs of child – healthy gene transferred and starts to work in child.

Disadvantages
- How far do scientists go?
- Do we clone human beings?
- Do we select the genes of our children? The moral debate will continue.

Tissue culture

A small group of cells taken from a plant or animal – grown using special media and chemicals such as hormones.

Examiner's tip
Be prepared to write a short essay to discuss advantages and disadvantages of genetic engineering.

Advantages
- Can produce thousands of identical plants from one small tissue culture.
- All plants genetically identical – clones.
- Human or animal cells also grown as tissue cultures – they don't form living things, just sheets of cells – can be used to test drugs etc. – saves using live animals.
- Embryo transplants carried out this way – fertilised ovum produces ball of cells – split up – each cell develops into an embryo on its own – vets use technique if farmer wants to produce lots of identical offspring in cattle, pigs or sheep.

Cloning

This is not quite genetic engineering – not altering genes – manipulating cells or cell nuclei – technique used in both plants and animals.

Examiner's tip
Be prepared to write a short essay on benefits and problems.

Problems
- Moral questions about human use of cultured embryos.
- Genes in clones all same – can cause problems.
- Lack of variation – evolutionary process has been stopped.
- Wild herds must be kept alive to maintain large number of natural genes for future generations to breed from.
- Cloning is quick and cheap way of breeding.

Selective breeding

- Humans use knowledge of genetics to select which animals and plants to breed.
- Right choice of animals to breed from could improve herd, e.g.
  - herds of cows that produce more milk
  - pigs that grow bigger
  - disease resistant cereals.

Evolution

- Evidence comes from **fossils** – found in rocks.
- Fossils show us how living things have changed – or stayed same – over millions of years.

Formation of fossils

- Hard parts of animals and plants – do not decay easily – covered by sand/silt – replaced over millions of years by minerals in rocks – animal/plant becomes rock – **fossil**.
- Sometimes soft tissues do not decay – reason? – microbes that cause matter to decay are absent or no oxygen to help decay process etc. – soft tissue then makes fossil.
- Life evolved over 3000 million years ago.
- Living things today evolved from living things from past – life evolved from first simple living things.
- Evolution takes millions of years – many animals and plants have become **extinct**.
- Changes in living things in fossil record – evidence that supports theory of evolution.

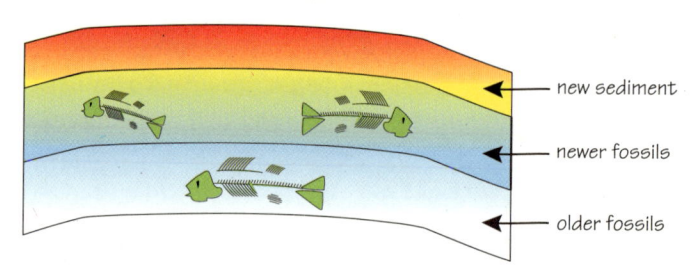

← new sediment
← newer fossils
← older fossils

Natural selection

How evolution happens.

- One species of living thing has many individual differences – differences are passed on in parents' genes – from generation to generation by reproduction.

Process of natural selection

- One characteristic very well suited to environment.
- May give that animal or plant and its offspring an advantage.
- Advantage (e.g. camouflage in an insect) means that animal survives – passes on its genes to its offspring.
- Over many generations camouflage may get better and species changes colour or shape – **evolution**.
- Characteristics suited to environment are passed on from one generation to next.
- Living things that 'fit' their environment will survive, those less well adapted could become extinct.

Questions

1. How many chromosomes are in a human cell nucleus? _____
2. What do you call the 'packages' of information on chromosomes? _____
3. What chemical are chromosomes made from? _____
4. How many chromosomes are there in a human sperm cell? _____
5. How many chromosomes are there in a human ovum? _____
6. What is the chromosome pair for sex determination in a human male? _____
7. What is the chromosome pair for sex determination in a human female? _____
8. Which word describes species of living things which no longer exist? _____

Use the words below to describe the following pairs of genes for questions 9 to 13.
homozygous recessive,   homozygous dominant,   heterozygous

If N is normal and C is recessive custic fibrosis gene:

9. The genotype CC is _____
10. The genotype NC is _____

If B = brown eyes and is dominant, b = blue eyes and is recessive

11. Bb _____
12. BB _____
13. bb _____
14. What gives us the most information about evolution? _____
15. By what process does evolution occur? _____
16. How long ago did life evolve on Earth? _____
17. What are genetically identical living things called? _____
18. What is the name of the process where humans control the breeding of animals? _____
19. What is the process of body cell division called? _____
20. What is the process of sex cell division called? _____
21. What do we call the process where genes are transferred from one living thing to another? _____
22. Which types of radiation cause mutations? _____

LIFE PROCESSES AND LIVING THINGS

Living things and their environment

Adaptation and competition

- Living things live where conditions suit them.
- They are in competition with each other.
- Population – group of animals or plants of same species living in same place.
- Community – group of populations of different species living in same place, e.g. pond, wood.

Population size

Population size may be affected by competition for/with:

- food – animals and plants compete for food resources – if successful, will survive to breed
- space and light – plants – photosynthesis needs light
  – animals – carnivore needs area to live in with enough prey animals for food – will often defend this area as its territory and drive away any other predators
- living things – herbivores restrict the growth and populations of plants
  – carnivores restrict populations of herbivores and other carnivores
- humans – can remove or introduce species – can affect whole food chain – effect may be devastating, e.g. grey squirrel vs. red squirrel
- disease – may deplete a population, e.g. myxomatosis kills rabbits.

Human impact on the environment

Air pollution

- Sulphur dioxide and nitrogen oxides.
- Produced when fossil fuels are burnt in furnaces and engines.
- These gases are dangerous – can cause asthma attacks.
- Gases dissolve in rain water to produce sulphuric acid and nitric acid – acid rain.
- This can kill plants – if acid content of rivers and lakes becomes too high, animals and plants cannot survive.

Increasing human population

- Raw materials – resources of Earth are being rapidly used up.
- Many resources are non-renewable.
- Greater standard of living – resources used faster.
- Leads to more waste – can lead to greater pollution unless there are adequate controls.

Management of Earth's resources and waste produced is one of the biggest problems to solve in the 21st century.

Water pollution

Polluted water can interfere with all of life's processes.

- Amount of O_2, nitrate, phosphate are indicators of water quality.

Pollutants

- Factory waste – may include acid, cyanide or metals such as mercury and lead.
- Acid irritates cells – damages plant roots, fish gills – prevents diffusion of oxygen – kills fish.
- Cyanide – poison of respiratory system – prevents cells from making energy – can kill in seconds – enters food chain.
- Mercury and lead affect bone and nerve cells.

Fertilisers

- Sprayed onto fields to increase crop production.
- Minerals are soluble – get washed away into rivers and lakes.
- Fertilisers increase growth of algae in water.
- Water turns green with algae in badly affected lake.
- Algae absorb light – stops it from reaching plants below surface.
- Bottom-living plants will die.
- Algae die off in winter.
- Dead plants decomposed by bacteria – uses oxygen from water.
- Water depleted in oxygen – animals suffocate and die.
- Bottom-living plants also hold mud with their roots – when they die a lot of mud and silt may be washed down to sea.
- River banks may collapse.
- Whole ecosystem of river or lake may be damaged.

Water becoming deoxygenated by decomposition of dead matter is called eutrophication. Polluting water with untreated sewage has the same effect.

Deforestation

- **Plants absorb carbon dioxide during photosynthesis.**
- **Release carbon dioxide** CO_2 during respiration – **absorb more than they give out**.
- Large numbers destroyed – level of CO_2 in air will increase.
- Wood is often burnt – releases more CO_2.
- Tropical rainforests contain enormous number of plants – are being destroyed at an alarming rate.
- Could mean more CO_2 remains in atmosphere.
- Could cause increased greenhouse effect – increase in temperature.

Greenhouse effect

- Earth is warm – has insulating layer – this traps some heat from Sun – prevents it from being re-radiated back into space – greenhouse effect.
- Water and carbon dioxide part of layer – absorb heat and radiate it back to Earth's surface.
- Has enabled life on Earth to survive.
- Recently has been giving cause for concern.
- Atmosphere has 0.03% of carbon dioxide – level, increasing over recent years – increased burning of fossil fuels – destruction of the tropical rainforests.
- Estimated that doubling CO^2 levels causes rise in temperature of 2 °C.
- Other gases trap heat as well – methane, some chlorofluorocarbons and nitrous oxides.
- Methane produced in intestines of cattle – also produced by rice plants as they grow.
- Producing more rice and beef or milk – increasing levels of methane in atmosphere – adding to greenhouse effect.

Increasing temperature may mean:
- changes in weather – problems with food production
- rise in sea level – problems in coastal areas for all living things – loss of environment.

Examiner's tip

Weigh up the evidence and form your own opinions. Be prepared to discuss it!

Use of ecosystems

- Organisms used by humans for food – crops grown – animals kept on farms and fish caught in sea.
- Stocks of wild animals used for food can be depleted, e.g. fishing – control number and size of fish caught – no control – fish population may crash – valuable food source lost for many years.

Careful management of natural stocks is needed and this may be achieved by governments co-operating to:

- agree quotas or limits on number of animals removed from wild each year
- be selective in which animals taken, e.g. only take non-breeding adult animals, not young or breeding animals
- avoid animal's breeding season – do not use breeding areas for fishing or hunting.

> **Examiner's tip**
> Be prepared to write a short essay on managing food production.

Artificial ecosystems

Those created by humans – amount of food produced in these areas kept very high by:
- using fertilisers
- using pesticides and fungicides to destroy pests
- reducing competition with wild animals and plants by various means
- bringing extra water by irrigation channels from reservoirs
- selectively breeding better animals and plants that are disease-resistant or grow bigger or faster
- using genetic engineering to produce disease-resistant crops.

Can have major effect on natural ecosystems – natural world needs consideration before farmland created.
All domestic animals need to be treated in humane way while growing, being transported and when killed.

Efficient artificial ecosystems

- Using short food chains – short food chain, less energy lost between links in chain.
- Food animals lose energy when move around – if movement restricted animals will grow faster – reason behind factory farming. Is it humane? Is it necessary?
- Controlling temperature – heating areas reduces heat lost by animals.

Energy and nutrient transfer

Producers

Sun is source of energy for all life on Earth.

- Green plants – capture the energy from Sun.
- Store energy in cells.
- Some energy used – growth and repair, making protein, fat etc.
- Some lost as waste.

Consumers

- Animals – some eat plants, some eat animals.
- Energy of plant or animal taken in.
- Energy used for repair, growth, making proteins, e.g. hormones, enzymes.
- Respiration produces energy for living processes.

- Energy lost in faeces – also as waste from chemical reactions in cells.
- Energy lost as heat – animals produce heat as they move – heat energy lost to air.
- **Mammals** and birds lose more energy this way – warm-blooded – homoiothermic.

Decomposers

- Microbes – bacteria and fungi.
- Dead materials completely decomposed – all energy originally captured by plant back into environment.

Pollution enters food chain

E.g.
- mercury builds up in plant tissue
- fish eat plants – mercury in diet
- mercury level builds up in fish – may kill fish
- fish eaten by predator, e.g. otter or pike
- these top consumers get high doses of mercury in diet – eventually kills them.

Often top consumer dies – levels of poison may not be high enough in producer or primary consumer – level increases further along the food chain you go – often reaches lethal levels at final predator.

Food webs

A food chain would be any single line from producer to top consumer

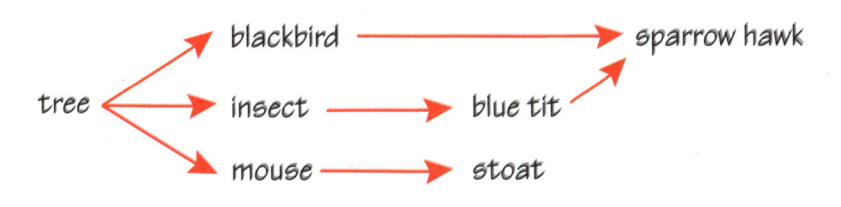

tree → blackbird → sparrow hawk
tree → insect → blue tit → sparrow hawk
tree → mouse → stoat

Pyramid of numbers
hawk / tit / insects / tree
One tree

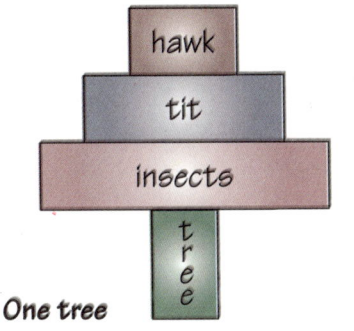

Pyramid of biomass
hawk / tit / insects / tree
Tree has large mass

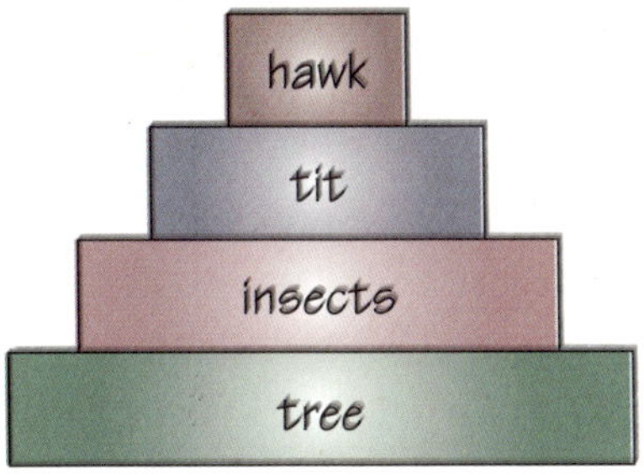

A large tree has a strange number pyramid - there is only one living thing at the base - not millions.

The size of each box in a pyramid represents the number of individuals or amount of biomass at that level.

Examiner's tip
You will need to know how to construct pyramids properly.

Use of microbes

Microbes

Fungi – include organisms as large as toadstools and as microscopically small as yeast.

- Cells of fungi have a cell wall – DNA is inside a nucleus.
- Yeast – used in brewing and baking industry – can be grown on simple media like agar.
- Other fungi like the mould penicillin – need vitamins to grow as well.
- Fungi are vital to the world – are the major decomposers of the dead material.
- Living things that decompose dead material are called saprophytes.
- Diseases caused include – Athlete's foot.

LIFE PROCESSES AND LIVING THINGS

Protozoa – single-celled – have membrane, nucleus and cytoplasm – vary from a simple **amoeba** to the complicated **paramecium**.

- Protozoa feed on bacteria and dead and decaying matter.
- Can cause disease, e.g. malaria (transmitted by mosquitoes) or diarrhoea – most are very useful to man – decomposing decayed matter.
- Used in sewage treatment.

Bacteria – much larger than viruses – more complex structures and a lot more DNA.

- Contain cytoplasm – surrounded by a thin membrane – DNA not inside a nucleus.
- Some are very hardy – will survive for years as spores until the conditions for growth are right, e.g. **anthrax**.
- Others cannot survive outside a living thing.
- Can reproduce outside cells and when they cause disease they destroy cells and use the contents for food.
- Bacterial **metabolism** produces **toxins** (poisons) which can cause the disease.
- Diseases caused by bacteria are: T.B., Whooping cough, Tetanus.
- Bacteria can be grown in culture (e.g. on agar plates) – culture contains food – soil bacteria may need only carbohydrate and minerals – disease-causing bacteria (pathogens) may need blood or protein together with vitamins if they are to grow in culture.
- All bacteria need water/moisture and some warmth to grow.
- Most bacteria are harmless to humans and are very beneficial.
- They decompose dead matter in the soil.
- In your intestine they help to digest your food and they make vitamins.
- They can be used to produce chemicals for our use, e.g. antibiotics, alcohol etc.

> **Examiner's tip**
> You need to be able to describe correct techniques for growing bacteria safely!

Viruses – small particles – made from protein and either DNA or RNA.

- Very few genes – gene for each protein – genes to control replication of virus inside the cell it invades.
- RNA viruses thought to be very primitive – may have been around since the first chemicals of life appeared on Earth.
- The most dangerous virus yet found is an RNA virus called **ebola** which is a **filovirus**.
- Viruses need a living cell in order to replicate – some can survive as crystals outside a cell for a long time.
- Diseases are caused by viruses: **polio**, **HIV**, **influenza**, **colds**, **chicken pox**.
- Viruses can be grown in cultures of **living cells**.

Killing germs
- Germicide – substance that kills microbes.
- Disinfectant – kills microbes on non-living material.
- Antiseptic – kills microbes on living tissues.
- Antibiotic – kills microbes on inside and outside of living things.

Biogas
- Mainly the gas methane.
- Microbes produce methane in large quantities as a result of anaerobic respiration.
- Food source of anaerobic respiration or sugar or carbohydrate.
- Fermentation is usually glucose or another sugar.
- Biogas generators can be used on a small scale – individual farms or villages – waste products can be used as energy source for microbes.

Carbon cycle

- **Carbon** in carbohydrate, protein and fat.
- Plants get their carbon from air – carbon dioxide (CO_2).
- Use it to make food – photosynthesis – build proteins, fats and carbohydrates.
- Animals get carbon by eating plants and other animals.
- Respiration – uses food – releases carbon dioxide back into air.
- Plants take in carbon dioxide – animals give out carbon dioxide.
- Plants and animals die – bodies decompose.
- Dead matter broken down by bacteria and other microbes – decomposers – carbon into their bodies.
- Decomposers also respire – carbon dioxide into air.
- Burning – releases carbon dioxide into air – extra carbon dioxide.

Examiner's tip
Important – must mention role of bacteria/fungi in C and N cycles.

Nitrogen cycle

- Nitrogen (N_2) needed to make proteins.
- Proteins build animal and plant tissue.
- Plants build proteins – take nitrate out of soil through roots.
- Animals eat plants – break down plant protein – build up animal protein.
- Animals excrete urea and faeces – contains nitrogen waste.
- Animals and plants die – the nitrogen can be returned to the cycle.
- Decomposing bacteria break the protein/urea/faeces down into ammonia (nitrogen + hydrogen).
- **Nitrifying bacteria** change this ammonia to nitrate (nitrogen + oxygen).
- Plant roots absorb nitrate – cycle again.
- **Denitrifying bacteria** – change nitrate into nitrogen gas.
- **Nitrogen-fixing bacteria** – take nitrogen out of air – build it into nitrates. These bacteria can be found by themselves in soil, or living in roots of plants belonging to pea and bean family, e.g. clover, peas etc. These plants are called legumes.

Learn this by drawing it yourself

Examiner's tip
Know basic information about fungi, protoctists, bacteria, viruses, killing germs.

LIFE PROCESSES AND LIVING THINGS

Questions

1. What is contained in fertiliser that seriously pollutes rivers? _____
2. Why do living things need carbon? _____
3. Why do living things need nitrogen? _____
4. Where do most plants get their nitrogen? _____
5. Where do herbivores get their nitrogen for amino acids? _____
6. Where do carnivores get their nitrogen? _____
7. What is the name of the microbes that change nitrate into nitrogen gas? _____
8. What is the name of the microbes that change nitrogen gas into nitrate? _____
9. What is the end product of urine breakdown by nitrifying bacteria? _____
10. Which raw materials are used by plants to make amino acids during photosynthesis? _____
11. Where do plants get their carbon from? _____
12. Where do animals get their carbon from? _____
13. What is the waste product of plant respiration? _____
14. What is the waste product of animal respiration? _____
15. What percentage of the air is carbon dioxide? _____
16. Which type of microbes live in the root nodules of legumes? _____
17. Which gas is mainly responsible for destructive 'acid rain'? _____
18. Which gases are responsible for the 'greenhouse effect'? _____
19. Rain is often naturally slightly acid. Which gas is responsible for 'natural' acid rain? _____
20. Which gases are the major pollutants from coal-fired power stations? _____
21. Which pollutant will damage the gills of fish? _____
22. Which poison prevents cells from making energy? _____
23. Which heavy metal has been linked to nerve damage in inner-city school children? _____
24. Which heavy metal can make bones very brittle as well as causing nerve damage? _____

Answers

Life processes and cell activity

1 Botany 2 Zoology 3 Sensitivity 4 Respiration 5 Excretion
6 Elimination or egestion 7 Reproduction 8 Growth 9 Oxygen
10 Respiration 11 Movement – respiration – sensitivity – feeding – excretion – reproduction – growth 12 MRS FERG 13 Cytoplasm 14 Nucleus
15 Cellulose cell wall 16 Chloroplast 17 Vacuole 18 Tissue 19 Organ
20 System 21 Organism 22 Vacuole – cellulose – chlorophyll 23 Cell
24 Organ 25 Organ

Humans as organisms

1 Carbohydrate, protein, fat 2 Peristalsis 3 Kills germs and creates best conditions for enzymes to work 4 Emulsifies fats – increases surface area of fat globules for enzymes to work on 5 Digests protein 6 Right ventricle
7 Left ventricle 8 Withstand high blood pressure 9 Keep blood travelling the right way – prevent backflow 10 Carry oxygen 11 Urea, carbon dioxide, dissolved food, hormones 12 Walls of alveoli 13 Aerobic 14 Anaerobic
15 Stimulus → receptor → co-ordinator → effector → response 16 Brain and spinal cord 17 Insulin 18 Glucagon 19 FSH 20 LH 21 Broken down to urea by liver 22 More permeable to water – water reabsorbed back into blood – concentrated urine produced 23 Bacteria – larger – more genes – can survive on their own. Viruses – much smaller – few genes + protein – only grow inside living cells 24 Nicotine

Green plants as organisms

1 Chlorophyll – in chloroplasts 2 Palisade mesophyll 3 Xylem 4 Phloem
5 Xylem 6 Bright light 7 Dark/cloudy 8 Warm/windy 9 Cold/wet/still
10 Summer 11 Diffusion 12 Osmosis 13 Turgid 14 Plasmolysed
15 Nitrate 16 Phosphate 17 Potassium 18 Potassium 19 Phosphate
20 Nitrate 21 Grow towards 22 Grow towards 23 Grow away

Variation, inheritance and evolution

1 46 2 Genes 3 DNA 4 23 5 23 6 XY 7 XX 8 Extinct
9 Homozygous recessive 10 Heterozygous 11 Heterozygous
12 Homozygous dominant 13 Homozygous recessive 14 Fossils
15 Natural selection 16 Over 3000 million years 17 Clones 18 Selective breeding 19 Mitosis 20 Meiosis 21 Genetic engineering 22 Ultra-violet, X-ray, gamma

Living things and their environment

1 Nitrate/phosphate 2 'building brick' of all molecules of life 3 To make proteins 4 Nitrate 5 Plants 6 Other animals 7 Denitrifiers
8 Nitrogen fixers 9 Ammonia 10 Nitrate, carbon dioxide, water 11 Carbon dioxide 12 Plants 13 Carbon dioxide 14 Carbon dioxide 15 0.03%
16 Nitrogen fixers 17 Sulphur dioxide 18 Carbon dioxide and methane
19 Carbon dioxide 20 Sulphur dioxide and nitrogen oxides 21 Sulphur dioxide as acid rain 22 Cyanide 23 Lead 24 Mercury

MATERIALS AND THEIR PROPERTIES

Classifying materials

Atomic structure

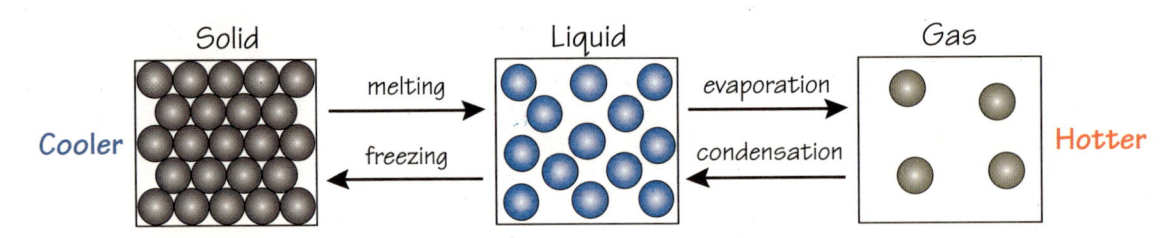

Solid → melting → Liquid → evaporation → Gas
Gas → condensation → Liquid → freezing → Solid

Cooler ← → Hotter

Evaporation occurs at any temperature.
Boiling occurs at the boiling point of a liquid and depends on pressure.

- **Solids** – fixed shape and volume – particles vibrate but cannot move about freely – strong forces of attraction between particles.
- **Liquid** – definite volume – particles close together but free to move within liquid – take shape of container – weaker forces of attraction between particles.
- **Gases** – fill container – particles free to move quickly and randomly within the space available (diffusion) – particles can be compressed into smaller volume – very weak forces of attraction.

Change of state

Solid → liquid → gas – heat energy makes particles vibrate more violently → forces become weaker → particles separate → free to move about.
- **Nucleus** has **protons** and **neutrons** – surrounded by **shells** containing **electrons**.

( ) = **maximum** number of **electrons**

nucleus
(2)
(8)
(8)

> **Complete** a shell before starting a new one.

> **Examiner's tip**
> Only electrons can change in chemical reactions.

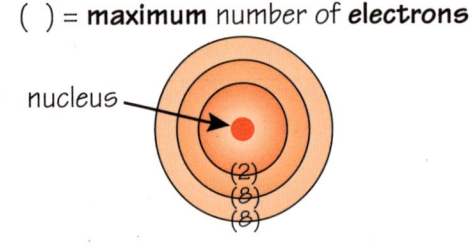

Shells fill from the **inside first**!
- Relative **charges** and **masses** of neutrons (n), protons (p) and electrons (e):

	Mass	Charge
p	1	+1
n	1	0
e	negligible	−1

- **Neutral atom** – number of protons **equals** number of electrons.
- **Atomic number** (proton number) – number of protons in nucleus – also **name/position** of element.
- **Mass number** – number of neutrons and protons **added** together.

> p and e different in ions.

Atoms represented by:
symbol e.g. $^{23}_{11}Na$ p = 11, n = 12 (23 - 11), e = 11
electron arrangement 2, 8, 1.

- Electrons in **outermost shell** is the group number (Na is **group 1**).
- Electrons in outer shell determine **reactivity** and **type** of reaction
  – metals lose electrons → positive ions
  – non-metals gain electrons → negative ions or share electrons with other atoms.
- **Isotopes** – same atomic number but **different** mass number
  – **same** number of protons, **different** number of neutrons.
  E.g. $^{35}_{17}Cl$ (p = 17, **n = 18**) $^{37}_{17}Cl$ (p = 17, **n = 20**)

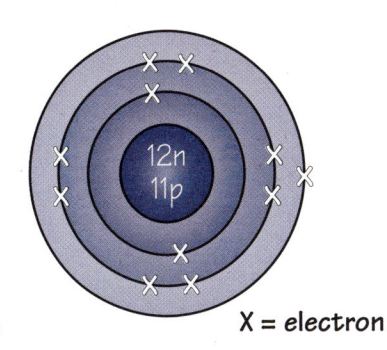

X = electron

Same chemical properties.

Bonding

- Atoms more stable when outer shell full – gain, lose or share electrons until outer shell full.
- Atoms combine by **bonding** to form new substances.

Two types bond:

Covalent
- between **non-metals**
- electrons **shared**.

Ionic
- between metal and **non-metal**
- electrons **transferred**.

*An **ion** is a **charged** atom.*

Dot and cross diagrams:

e.g. **methane** (CH_4)

e.g. **sodium chloride** (NaCl)

Examiner's tip
Only need to draw **outer** shells when showing bonding.

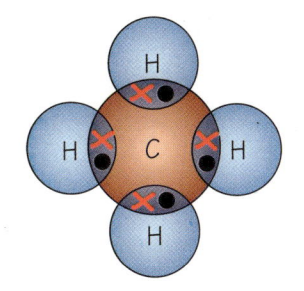

x = C electron   • = H electron
C in group 4 (4e in outer shell)

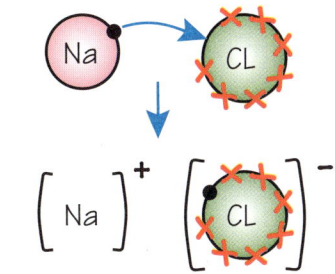

Na loses 1 electron
charge **+1** as 1 **more** p than e

Cl **gains** 1 electron
charge **–1** as 1 **more** e than p

- Bonding causes atoms to become **more stable** by achieving the electron arrangement of a **noble gas**.
- **Properties of compounds** related to **strengths** of attractions **between** particles.
- **Giant ionic** – **strong** electrostatic attractions in **lattice**
  – lead to high melting point (m.pt) and high boiling point (b.pt).

Noble gases have full outer electron shells e.g. He 2 Ne 2,8 Ar 2,8,8.

MATERIALS AND THEIR PROPERTIES

E.g. NaCl

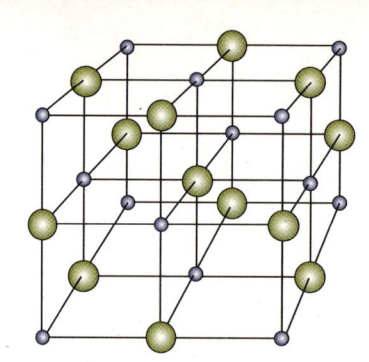

○ = Na⁺
● = Cl⁻

- **Covalent** – can be **giant molecular** – SiO_2 (sand), graphite, diamond – large number of bonds in structure
  – or **simple molecular** – NH_3, H_2O.
- **Graphite** – layered structure → weak forces between layers → layers can slide → lubricant → each C forms 3 covalent bonds → mobile electrons → electrical conduction.

- Diamond – each C forms 4 bonds → rigid structure.
- No mobile electrons → no electrical conduction.

All electrons form covalent bonds. None is mobile.

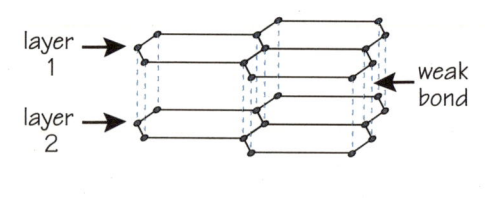

layer 1
layer 2
weak bond

graphite   diamond   ● = C atom

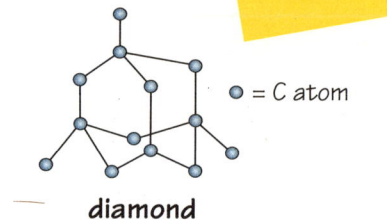

Properties

Property	Giant ionic	Giant molecular	Simple molecular
m.pt/b.pt	high	high	low
states	solid	solid	solid, liquid or gas
solubility in water	good	poor	poor
solubility in organic solvent	poor	poor	good
electrical conduction	yes (**molten/aqueous** only)	no (**except graphite**)	no

- Note: **strong** covalent bonds **between atoms** but **weak** attractions **between molecules** in molecular substances lead to low m.pt and b.pt.

Metallic bonding

Positive ions in a sea of electrons – **more delocalised mobile electrons** → stronger bonding.
- Outer shell electron of metal atom – free to move through structure – allows metals to conduct heat and electricity.
- Electrons hold atoms in a very strong regular structure.
- High melting/boiling points.
- Atoms slide over each other → malleable and ductile.

E.g. structure of sodium:

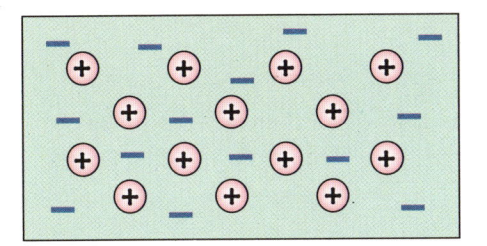

⊕ = sodium ion

— = delocalised electrons

Alloys

- Usually **mixture** of metals.
- Different-sized atoms prevent slip → hard metals.
- Less dense – more space between atoms created by large atom.

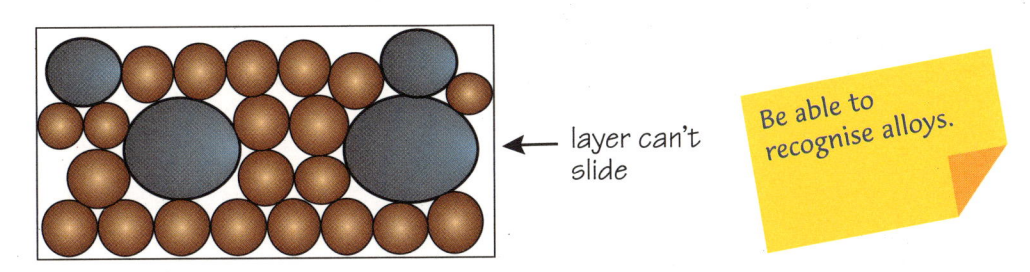

← layer can't slide

Be able to recognise alloys.

- E.g. (a) steel: iron, carbon, nickel, manganese, chromium
  (b) dental filling: mercury, silver, iron.

Questions

1 (a) Complete the table below:

Particle	Mass Number	Number of Protons	Number of Neutrons	Number of Electrons	Electron Arrangement
Li atom		3	4		
Li$^+$ ion					
^{12}C isotope	12			6	
^{13}C isotope	13	6			
Ne atom			10	10	
S^{2-} ion	32			18	

(b) Which of the above particles have the inert gas electron arrangement?
_____

2 Draw an aluminium atom $^{27}_{13}$Al.

3 Draw a diagram to show the bonding between $^{24}_{12}$Mg and $^{16}_{8}$O.

4 All atoms of the same element contain the same number of _____ and _____.

5 Study this table:

	Melting point	Conducts when solid	Conducts when molten
A	high	yes	yes
B	low	no	no
C	high	no	yes

(a) Which could be aluminium? _____

(b) Which could be sodium chloride? _____

(c) Which could be water? _____

Patterns of behaviour

Periodic Table

- **Periodic Table** – elements arranged in increasing atomic number.

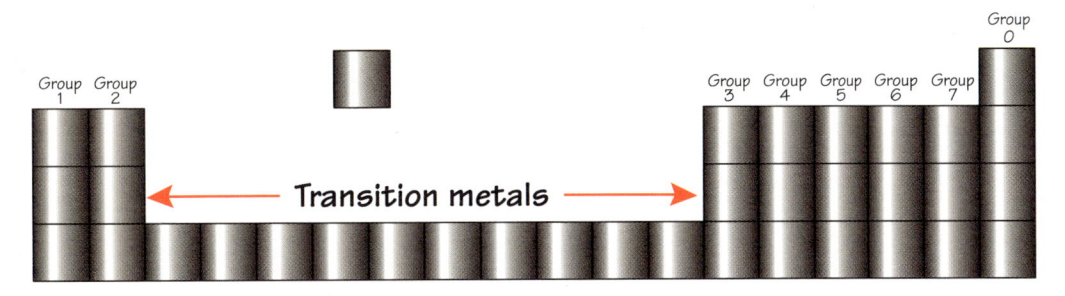

- Elements with similar properties are in groups (columns) – have same number of electrons in outer shell.
- Gradual change in property and reactivity from top of group to bottom.
- Metals more reactive at bottom of group.
- Non-metals more reactive at top of group.
- Metals in groups 1, 2 and 3 – form positive ions.
- Non-metals in groups 5, 6, 7 – form negative ions.
- Group 8 (O) – chemically unreactive – exist as single atoms.

Learn trends

Group 1 trends
less reactive metal

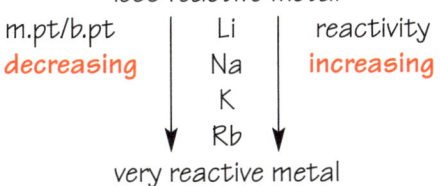

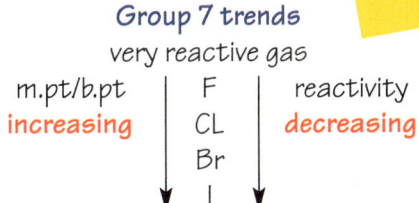

m.pt/b.pt | Li | reactivity
decreasing | Na | increasing
| K |
| Rb |

very reactive metal

Group 7 trends
very reactive gas

m.pt/b.pt | F | reactivity
increasing | Cl | decreasing
| Br |
| I |

unreactive solid

Group 1 - alkali metals

- Metals stored under oil – very reactive.
- React violently with water making hydrogen gas and alkaline solutions:
  $2Li(s) + 2H_2O(l) \rightarrow 2LiOH(aq) + H_2(g)$

- Metals move on surface of water, cloudy solution – pH > 12.
- React with non-metals to form ionic compounds – metal carries a +1 charge.
- Shiny when cut but tarnish rapidly in air (oxygen):
  i.e. $4Li(s) + O_2(g) \rightarrow 2Li_2O(s)$.

Examiner's tip
Learn the reactions of **one** element in each group.

Properties and uses of alkali metal compounds

- Are ionic – high m.pt / b.pt, soluble in water, conduct in molten/aqueous form.
- NaCl – making chlorine, sodium hydroxide and hydrogen (electrolysis), gritting roads, diet.

Group 7 - halogens

- Non-metals – exist as molecules with 2 atoms (diatomic) – Cl–Cl.
- Have coloured vapours (F_2 – pale yellow, Cl_2 – pale green, Br_2 – red/orange, I_2 – purple) – colour darkens down the group.

- Form ionic salts with metals – halogen atom carries a –1 charge (halide ion).
- Corrosive and toxic.

Similar property – same number of electrons in outer shell (energy level) – higher it is in the group the more easily it gains electrons:
- fluorine readily gains electrons to give F^- – strong oxidising agent
- iodine less readily gains electrons to give I^- – weak oxidising agent.

Reactions of halogens

- More reactive element displaces less reactive ion from solution, e.g. F_2 will displace Cl^- but Br_2 will not displace Cl^- ions:

$$F_2(g) + 2Cl^-(aq) \rightarrow 2F^-(aq) + Cl_2(g)$$
$$Cl_2(g) + 2Br^-(aq) \rightarrow 2Cl^-(aq) + Br_2(l)$$

Reactivity explained.

Can put other elements into reactivity order by displacement.

Uses of halogens

- Water purification, making bleaches, disinfectants, pesticides, antiseptics.

Uses of halogen compounds

- Silver halides – photography.
- Fluorides – tooth pastes and water supply.
- NaCl as above.

Properties and uses of group 8 (0) - noble gases

- Have full outer electron shells.
- Very unreactive gases – exist as single atoms.
- Ar – in filament bulbs.
- Ne – electrical discharge tubes (sign making).
- He – air ships (balloons).

Transition metals

Between groups 2 and 3 – they:
- have high m.pt/b.pt, high densities and very hard – strong – used in construction, e.g. iron and alloys
- form coloured compounds
- act as catalysts, e.g.
  Ni – making margarines
  Pt – oxidation of ammonia to make nitric acid
  Fe – Haber process – making ammonia
  V_2O_5 – contact process – makes sulphuric acid
- have compounds used in paints and dyes, breathalysers, cereals, medicines.

These are transition metals.

Questions

1. Study the section of the Periodic Table below and answer the questions which follow.

																	G
													E				
	C															F	
D		A			B												

(a) Which of the above elements are metals? _____

(b) Which element has atomic number 6? _____

(c) Which element forms an oxide which dissolves in water and turns universal indicator solution purple? _____

(d) Write a chemical equation for the reaction of Ca with oxygen. _____

2. (a) The element sodium (Na) is found in group _____ called the_____ _____. The metal is stored _____ _____ because it _____ violently with _____.

   (b) A small piece of sodium is added to water. Describe what you will see happening.
   _____
   _____

3. The element Fe is used as a catalyst in the _____ process for making _____.

4. Ne and Ar are called _____ _____ because they do not _____ with anything else. They are found in group_____.

5. Bromine (Br) in group _____ called the _____ is less reactive than chlorine.

   Chlorine gas was bubbled into an aqueous solution containing bromide ions. Write an ionic equation for the reaction. _____
   This reaction is called a _____ _____.

6. List three ways in which transition metals differ from group 1 metals.
   _____
   _____

7. From the list: bromine, chlorine, iodine, silver bromide and sodium chloride, give:

   (a) a halogen which is a liquid at room temperature. _____

   (b) a chemical found in sea water but not in fresh water. _____

   (c) a substance broken down by light. _____

MATERIALS AND THEIR PROPERTIES

43

Changing materials

This section provides notes on:
- **extraction** – obtaining metals from their ores
- **synthesis** – building new substances from elements or simpler compounds.
  Examples – extracting iron from iron ore, and aluminium from bauxite.
  – synthesising ammonia (NH_3) from nitrogen and hydrogen.

- **Raw material** – substance which occurs **naturally** (**in nature**) – may not be starting materials for the chemical reaction.

Some important points about extracting metals from their ores:
- **ores** – are either metal oxides or substances which can be changed into metal oxides, usually by roasting
- **reduction** – removal of oxygen from oxides leaving metal.

Reduction method depends upon position of metal in activity series.
- Metals **high** in series – e.g. sodium, calcium, aluminium – can only be reduced by **electrolysis**.
- Metals **low** in series – e.g. iron, copper – can be reduced using **carbon** or **carbon monoxide** or **by more reactive metal**, e.g. Zn.

Examiner's tip
Always describe industrial processes.

Extracting iron from iron ore

- **Iron ore** usually used is **haematite** – Fe_2O_3.
- **Raw materials** are **haematite** (Fe_2O_3), coke (C), **limestone** ($CaCO_3$).
- Limestone added to remove impurities such as sand (SiO_2).
- Energy from hot gases removed to save energy/cost.

Examiner's tip
Very common question.

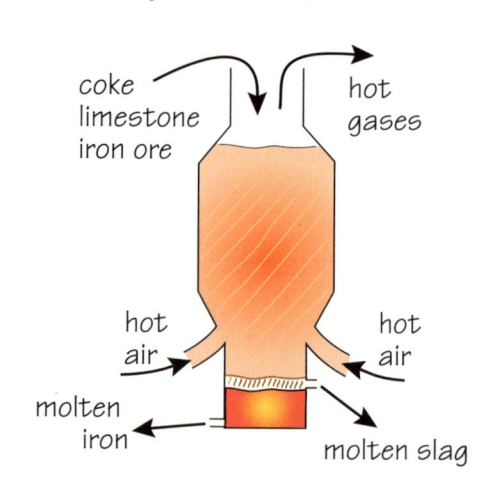

Blast furnace

The process
- Iron, coke and limestone are crushed, mixed and loaded into top of furnace.
- A blast of very hot air is blown into mixture to make reaction work.
- **Coke burns in hot air** (**oxygen**) → **carbon dioxide** + **heat**.
- **Carbon dioxide reacts with more coke** → **carbon monoxide**.
- **Carbon monoxide reduces (removes) oxygen from haematite** → **iron**.
- **Limestone reacts with sand and other impurities** → **slag**.
- **Molten iron sinks to bottom**.
- **Molten slag floats on the iron**.

Equations for the reaction:
coke + oxygen → carbon dioxide + heat
$C(s) + O_2(g) \rightarrow CO_2(g)$
This reaction **gives out heat** – **exothermic**.

carbon dioxide + coke → carbon monoxide
$$CO_2(g) + C(s) → 2CO(g)$$

carbon monoxide + haematite → iron + carbon dioxide
$$3CO(g) + Fe_2O_3(s) → 2Fe(l) + 3CO_2(g)$$

limestone + sand → slag + carbon dioxide
$$CaCO_3(s) + SiO_2(s) → CaSiO_3(l) + CO_2(g)$$

> You must be able to write balanced equations.

> Reactive element will displace less reactive one.

Making steel
- Iron from blast furnace is brittle – called cast iron.
- **Cast iron** is converted into steel by removing excess carbon.
- **Oxygen** is blown through cast iron to burn carbon away.
- Sometimes small amounts of other metals, e.g. nickel, manganese, chromium, added to produce an alloy (mixture) – produce a special steel such as stainless steel.

Uses of slag
- Insulation, road building, building materials.

Electrolysis

- **Breaking down a substance containing ions**, e.g. molten compound or aqueous solution using electricity. Very expensive method.

Some important points about electrolysis
- Substance must be in molten (melted/fused) state or dissolved in water.
- **Direct current** needed – causes ion movement.
- Ions are free to move about in the molten or aqueous form.
- Electrodes – ions are discharged.
- **Not** AC – no ion movement.

Common substances which can undergo electrolysis
- All aqueous acids/alkalis.
- Ionic compounds, e.g. NaCl, Al_2O_3.
- **Generally covalent compounds do not conduct**.

Apparatus needed

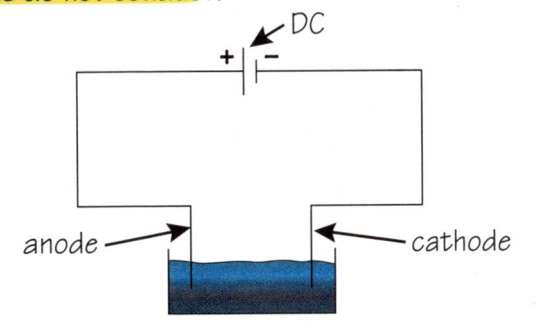

(diagram: DC source connected to anode and cathode in an electrolyte)

Comparison between electrolysis and conduction in a wire

Electrolysis
ions carry the current
substance broken down
no current when no ions left

Conduction (wire)
electrons carry the current
no change to wire
current passes indefinitely

> **Examiner's tip**
> Give clear unambiguous answers.

MATERIALS AND THEIR PROPERTIES

Electrolysis - extracting reactive metals

- **Groups 1, 2 and 3** of Periodic Table.
- **Molten/fused purified metal compounds used.**
- **Salts added** (e.g. cryolite) → lower melting point → increase electrical conductivity → economical.

Extracting aluminium from bauxite (Al_2O_3)
- Large quantity of electricity used.

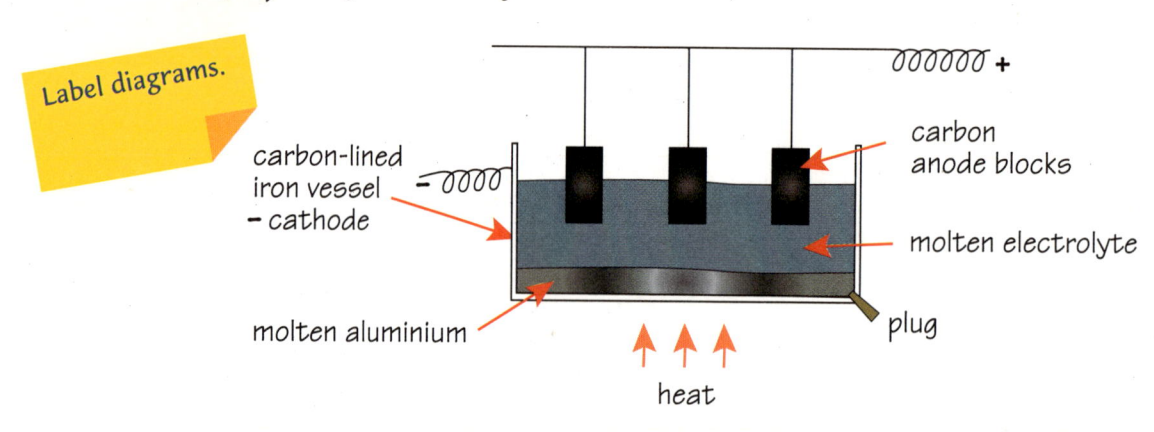

Label diagrams.

Diagram labels: carbon-lined iron vessel – cathode; carbon anode blocks; molten electrolyte; molten aluminium; plug; heat.

- Plants are built near power source and coast.
- **Raw materials** are bauxite and cryolite.
- Carbon (graphite) electrodes with large surface area → speed up discharge.
- They are cheap and abundant.

Ionic equations for the reactions
Cathode:
$$Al^{3+}(l) + 3e^- \rightarrow Al_{(l)}$$
Al^{3+} reduced since it gains electrons.

Anode:
$$2O^{2-}_{(l)} - 4e^- \rightarrow O_2(g)$$
or use
$$2O^{2-}_{(l)} \rightarrow O_2(g) + 4e^-$$
O^{2-} oxidised since it loses electrons.

Examiner's tip: Both versions OK.

Carbon anodes react with hot oxygen – erodes them – need replacing regularly otherwise discharge rate low.

$$C(s) + O_2(g) \rightarrow CO_2(g)$$

- **Molten aluminium tapped off** → allowed to cool → useful materials made.
- Relate main property to its application.

Examiner's tip: Be precise with use and always give 2 unrelated uses.

Uses of aluminium	Property
cooking utensils	good conductor of heat – doesn't corrode or melt
overhead electric cables	good electrical conductor – low density → light
window frames	strong and doesn't corrode
aeroplanes	strong and low density → light

Purification of metals by electrolysis

- Extractions not involving electrolysis form impure metals.
- 99+ % pure by electrolysis.

The process:
- impure metal makes anode
- pure metal cathode – rotated
- low DC current
- electrolyte contains metal ions of impure metal
- impurities drop to bottom of vessel
- cathode increases in size
- anode decreases in size.

Example: purification of copper metal

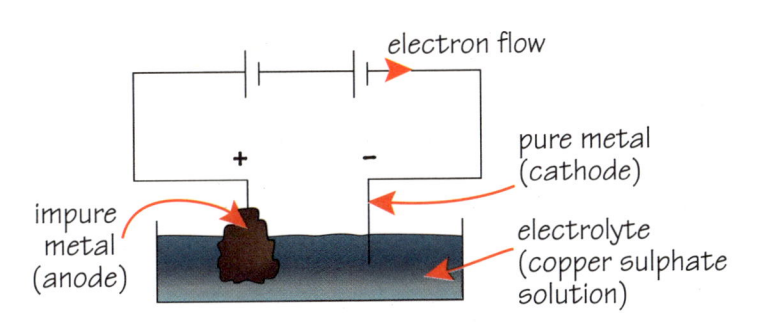

- Same set-up for electroplating objects – object to be coated is at cathode.

Ionic equations for the reactions

Anode
$$Cu(s) \rightarrow Cu^{2+}(aq) + 2e^-$$
copper metal loses electrons → oxidised to Cu^{2+} ions.

Cathode
$$Cu^{2+}(aq) + 2e^- \rightarrow Cu(s)$$
copper ion (Cu^{2+}) gains electrons → reduced to Cu metal.

As REDuction and OXidation happen together – REDOX reactions.

The following **observations** are made when copper is purified:
- **blue electrolyte stays same colour intensity throughout**
- **pink deposit on cathode → larger cathode**
- **container heats up during electrolysis**
- **anode gets smaller**
- **impurities under anode.**

Examiner's tip

If asked to describe what you see – say what you see – don't just name the substances.

MATERIALS AND THEIR PROPERTIES

47

Useful products from air

Haber process - ammonia ($NH_3(g)$)

- Ammonia – raw material for making nitric acid, fertilisers, plastics etc.

Raw materials are air and natural gas.
Equation for reaction:
$$N_2(g) + 3H_2(g) \rightleftharpoons 2NH_3(g) \quad \Delta H = -93 \text{ kJ/mole}$$

Starting materials:
- nitrogen (N_2) – fractional distillation of liquid air
- hydrogen (H_2) from natural gas (CH_4) – reaction with steam at high temperature and pressure catalyst
$$CH_4(g) + H_2O(g) \rightarrow CO(g) + 3H_2(g).$$

Note difference between raw and starting materials.

- Reaction is reversible.
- At equilibrium, speed of both reactions is equal.
- Occurs in closed container – (nothing leaves or enters the container).
- Industrial processes do not reach equilibrium (time-consuming and costly).
- Concentration depends on reaction conditions.
- Le Chatelier's principle explains how conditions affect amounts of reactants and products.

Conditions for high yield (amount) of ammonia:

Predicted	Actual
high pressure	high pressure (200 atm)
low temperature	moderately high temperature (450°C)
remove ammonia	remove ammonia
catalyst	catalyst (iron/iron oxide)

Learn actual conditions

The process
- Gases leaving – mixture of ammonia and unchanged nitrogen and hydrogen.
- Gases are cooled until ammonia (b.pt −33°C) condenses.
- Unreacted hydrogen and nitrogen recycled.

Le Chatelier's principle

Learn to apply this 'law'.

Whatever you do to the equilibrium, it does opposite, e.g. increase in temperature – equilibrium will try to decrease the temperature.

Explanations for chosen conditions
We can make predictions using Le Chatelier's principle:
- endothermic reaction – temperature increased – yield of product increases
- exothermic reaction, e.g. (making ammonia) – temperature increased – yield of product decreases.

Understand the temperature anomaly:
- low temperature **should** give high yield
- molecules have **lower energy** than **activation energy** barrier
- so **collisions unsuccessful** or very slow reaction → **low yield**.

Examiner's tip
Examiners are keen on this.

direction of equilibrium with **decreased** temperature
$$N_2(g) + 3H_2(g) \rightleftharpoons 2NH_3(g) + \text{heat}$$
direction of equilibrium with **increased** temperature

Pressure effect:
- pressure increase
- number of particles (moles) decreases
- equilibrium moves forming fewer particles
- vice versa

direction of equilibrium with **increased** pressure
$$N_2(g) + 3H_2(g) \rightleftharpoons 2NH_3(g)$$
direction of equilibrium with **decreased** pressure

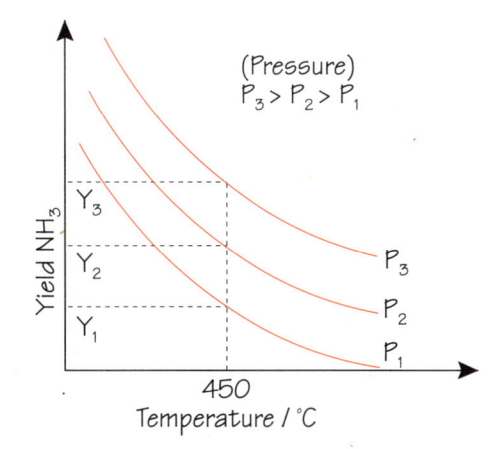

- yield higher for a higher pressure at fixed temperature ($Y_3 > Y_2 > Y_1$).

E.g. for ammonia: from equation
4 moles of gas on left makes **2 moles of gas** on right.

Concentration effect:
- **increase** in reactant concentration → **increase** in products
- **removing** products → **decrease** in reactants
- factors are **optimised** in industrial process – so time and energy are **not wasted**.

E.g. for ammonia:
- temperature **raised** – allowing **successful collisions** – but **yield** goes **down**
- **balance** – reasonable **rate** (**speed**) and adequate **yield** (see above graph)
- ammonia yield – **11–14%**
- **unreacted** nitrogen and hydrogen **recycled** – effective yield 100%.

Note 10°C increase in temperature = rate doubles.

E_A – activation energy barrier

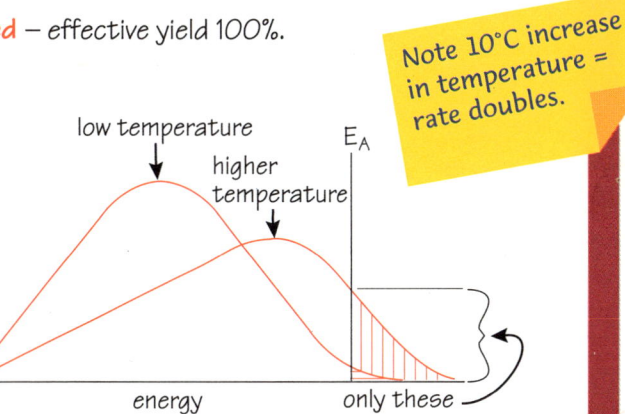

only these molecules react

Fertilisers

Help to provide an adequate and rapid food supply:
- **increasing human population** → needs more food → fertilisers provide **essential elements**, e.g. N, for growing crops → increased yields
- **plants cannot use nitrogen gas** → soluble forms needed by roots → nitrates or ammonium salts.

The process:
- **ammonia oxidised** → **nitrogen oxides** $NO_2(g)$
- **nitrogen oxides react with oxygen and water** → **nitric acid**
- **nitric acid neutralises ammonia or ammonia solution** → ammonium nitrate fertilisers
- **sulphuric/hydrochloric acid neutralises ammonia** or ammonia solution → fertilisers, e.g. ammonium sulphate and ammonium chloride.

> **Examiner's tip**
> Learn this one.

Conversion of ammonia to nitric acid – equations for reactions:
ammonia + oxygen → nitrogen oxide + water (platinum catalyst at 900°C)
$$4NH_3(g) + 5O_2(g) \rightarrow 4NO(g) + 6H_2O(g)$$

nitrogen oxide + oxygen → nitrogen dioxide (brown gas)
$$2NO(g) + O_2(g) \rightarrow 2NO_2(g)$$

This reaction is **very fast**.

nitrogen dioxide + oxygen + water → nitric acid
$$4NO_2(g) + O_2(g) + 2H_2O(l) \rightarrow 4HNO_3(l)$$

- Nitric acid – typical strong acid – fully dissociated – pH <1.
- Ammonia dissolves in water to make **ammonia solution**
  $$NH_3(g) + H_2O(l) \rightleftharpoons NH_4^+(aq) + OH^-(aq)$$
- Contains ammonium ions (NH_4^+) and **hydroxide ions** (OH^-).
- **Partly dissociated** – a **weak** base (pH9 – only a **few OH^- ions** are formed).

Neutralisation of acids

Ionic equation for neutralisation process:

$$H^+(aq) + OH^-(aq) \rightarrow H_2O(l)$$

> Application of process important.

- Strong acids are **fully dissociated** – high **H^+ ion** concentration – low pH.
- **With ammonia solution** – forms **nitrogenous fertilisers**.

Equations for the reactions:
acid + alkali → salt + water

e.g.

hydrochloric acid + ammonia solution → ammonium chloride + water
$$HCl(aq) + NH_4OH(aq) \rightarrow NH_4Cl(aq) + H_2O(l)$$

nitric acid + ammonia solution → ammonium nitrate + water
$$HNO_3(aq) + NH_4OH(aq) \rightarrow NH_4NO_3(aq) + H_2O(l)$$

sulphuric acid + ammonia solution → ammonium sulphate + water
$$H_2SO_4(aq) + 2NH_4OH(aq) \rightarrow (NH_4)_2SO_4(aq) + 2H_2O(l)$$

Solid fertilisers made by **evaporation** of neutralised solution.

> **Examiner's tip**
> Learn detailed method for preparation.

Higher percentage of nitrogen in fertiliser (see table) **the better as:**
- more effective for plant growth
- less needed – easier storage and transportation.

Fertiliser	Formula	Mass of one mole	Mass N in one mole	% of N
ammonium chloride	NH_4Cl	53.5 g	14 g	$\frac{14}{53.5} \times 100 = 26$
ammonium nitrate	NH_4NO_3	80 g	28 g	$\frac{28}{80} \times 100 = 35$
ammonium sulphate	$(NH_4)_2SO_4$	132 g	28 g	$\frac{28}{132} \times 100 = 21$

Problems with excessive use of fertiliser:
- may alter the pH of soil
- run off into rivers/lakes → eutrophication
- contamination of drinking water → blue baby syndrome and cancer
- harm animals and destroy crumb structure of soil.

Sulphuric acid: the Contact process

Raw materials: sulphur, air and water.

The process

- Sulphur is burnt in air → sulphur dioxide.
- Sulphur dioxide reacts with more air → sulphur trioxide.
- Sulphur trioxide reacts with concentrated sulphuric acid (98%) → oleum.
- Oleum reacts with water → sulphuric acid.

Equilibrium reaction.

Can cause pollution → acid rain.

Equations for the reactions:
sulphur burns in air:
$$S(g) + O_2(g) \rightarrow SO_2(g)$$

sulphur dioxide + air + vanadium (V) oxide catalyst → sulphur trioxide
$$2SO_2(g) + O_2(g) \rightleftharpoons 2SO_3(g) \quad \Delta H = \text{exothermic}$$

Equilibrium conditions: 450°C, 1 atm (see Haber process page 50 for reasons)

Pressure increases yield but it is already 98% so not worth the extra cost.

sulphur trioxide + sulphuric acid → oleum
$$SO_3(g) + H_2SO_4(l) \rightarrow H_2S_2O_7(l)$$

oleum + water → sulphuric acid
$$H_2S_2O_7(l) + H_2O(l) \rightarrow 2H_2SO_4(aq)$$

Note: sulphur trioxide not dissolved directly into water → fine mist.

Reactions of dilute sulphuric acid to make salts

Salts → hydrogen in acid replaced by a metal.

Methods: reacts with
- reactive metals → salt + hydrogen
  $Mg(s) + H_2SO_4(aq) \rightarrow MgSO_4(aq) + H_2(g)$

  Above hydrogen in series.

- metal carbonates → salt + water + carbon dioxide
  $CuCO_3(s) + H_2SO_4(aq) \rightarrow CuSO_4(aq) + H_2O(l) + CO_2(g)$

  Same reactions with other acids.

- metal oxides → salt + water
  $MgO(s) + H_2SO_4(aq) \rightarrow MgSO_4(aq) + H_2O(l)$

- alkali → salt + water (**neutralisation**)
  $2NaOH(aq) + H_2SO_4(aq) \rightarrow Na_2SO_4(aq) + 2H_2O(l)$

- hydrogen carbonates → salt + water + carbon dioxide
  $2NaHCO_3(s) + H_2SO_4(aq) \rightarrow Na_2SO_4(aq) + 2H_2O(l) + 2CO_2(g)$

Ionic equation: $H^+(aq) + OH^-(aq) \rightarrow H_2O(l)$

Use **titration** method → how much of the two solutions will just react → **indicator** → end point (phenolphthalein; pink in alkali → colourless in acid).

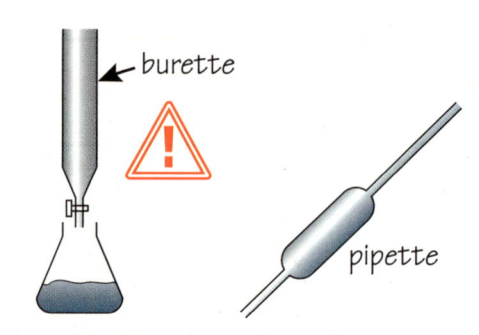

Example of calculation:
25 cm³ of 0.1 mol/dm³ HCl just react with 25 cm³ NaOH. What is the concentration of NaOH?

- balanced equation for reaction: NaOH + HCl → NaCl + H2O
  ratio   1   :   1
- 25 cm³ 0.1 mol/dm³ HCl contains $\frac{25 \times 0.1}{1000} = 0.0025$ moles
- moles of NaOH present in 25 cm³ = 0.0025 as ratio 1:1
- concentration of NaOH = $\frac{0.0025 \times 1000}{25} = 0.1$ mol/dm³

Precipitation

Two soluble salts mixed → soluble salt + insoluble salt (precipitate)
e.g. sodium chloride + silver nitrate → sodium nitrate + silver chloride (insoluble)
$NaCl(aq) + AgNO_3(aq) \rightarrow NaNO_3(aq) + AgCl(s)$
(see halogens (group 7) page 43)

Note: all group 1 salts and all nitrate compounds, including lead and silver, are soluble; most carbonates, except group 1, are insoluble.

Examiner's tip
General rule.

Reaction of concentrated sulphuric acid

Dehydrating/drying agent → remove water/or elements of water from substance
Dehydrating agent, e.g. water:
- e.g. (a) hydrated blue copper (II) sulphate crystal → white anhydrous copper (II) sulphate powder + water

  $CuSO_4 \cdot 5H_2O(s) \rightarrow CuSO_4(s) + 5H_2O(g)$

- **water of crystallisation is lost**

  (b) sugar → carbon + water

  $C_6H_{12}O_6(s) \rightarrow 6C(s) + 6H_2O(g)$

use as test for water

- **hydrogen** and oxygen removed from compound as water.

  Oxidising agent sulphuric acid: reduced to sulphur dioxide gas

  copper + sulphuric acid → copper sulphate + sulphur dioxide + water

- $Cu(s) + 2H_2SO_4(l) \rightarrow CuSO_4(aq) + SO_2(g) + 2H_2O(l)$
  oxidised   reduced

- carbon + sulphuric acid → carbon dioxide + sulphur dioxide + water

  $C(s) + 2H_2SO_4(l) \rightarrow CO_2(g) + 2SO_2(g) + 2H_2O(l)$
  oxidised   reduced

Acids and alkalis

Substances which dissolve in water to form solutions which are: acid or alkaline or neutral.
- pH – concentration of hydrogen ions (H^+) in solution.

Acids

- High (H^+) → low pH → strong acid → fully ionised → only ions present
  e.g. sulphuric, hydrochloric and nitric acid

  $HCl(g) + H_2O(l) \rightarrow H^+(aq) + Cl^-(aq)$

  pH = 1 or 2.

- Low (H^+) → higher pH → weak acid → partially ionised → few ions formed → equilibrium
  e.g. methanoic and ethanoic acid

  $CH_3COOH(l) + H_2O(l) \rightleftharpoons H^+(aq) + CH_3COO^-(aq)$

  These have pH = 3 or 4.

  ionisation determines strength

  Note: 0.1 M HCl acid and 0.1 M ethanoic acid → both **same concentration** → same number of particles.
  But **HCl is stronger** acid than ethanoic acid → **fully ionised** – ethanoic is partially ionised.

Alkalis

- Strong alkali → pH > 12 → fully ionised → hydroxide ions (OH^-) formed
  e.g. sodium hydroxide

  $NaOH(s) + H_2O(l) \rightarrow Na^+(aq) + OH^-(aq)$

- Weak alkali → pH < 12 → partially ionised → few hydroxide ions formed,
  e.g. ammonia solution pH = 9

  $NH_3(g) + H_2O(l) \rightleftharpoons NH_4^+(aq) + OH^-(aq)$

Indicators

Colour change of indicator shows type of solution made.

		Colour	
Indicator	**acid**	**alkali**	**neutral**
universal	red	purple	green
blue litmus	red	blue	blue (no change)
red litmus	red	blue	red (no change)
phenolpthalein	colourless	pink	colourless

Strength of solution measured on pH scale:

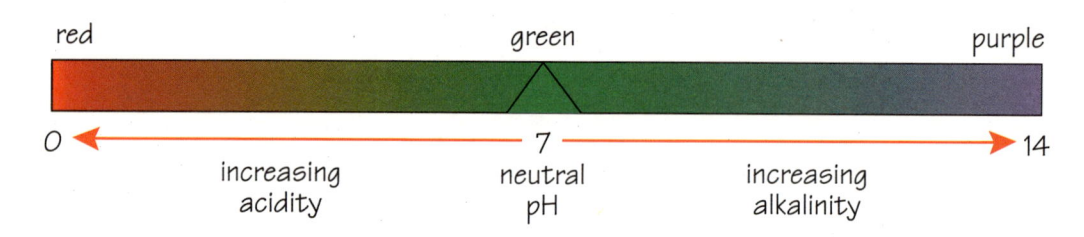

red — green — purple
0 ←——— 7 ———→ 14
increasing acidity — neutral pH — increasing alkalinity

- acids pH < 7
- alkali pH > 7
- **low** pH → **strong** acid
- **high** pH → **strong** alkali.

Rusting

Rust – hydrated iron (III) oxide (Fe_2O_3) – reddish/brown.
Metals react with air – **corrosion**.
Iron corrodes → rusting – weakens metal – expensive to repair.

Rusting caused by:
- oxygen
- water
- acids
- salty water/high temperatures.

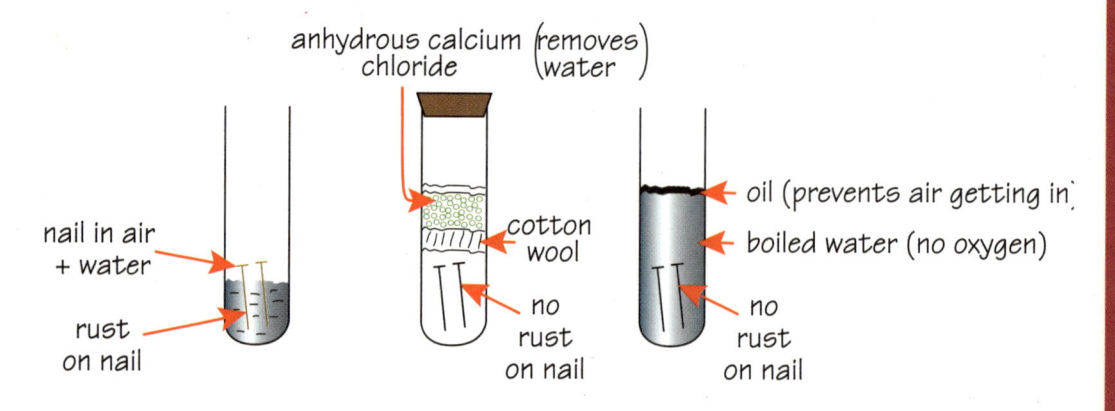

Experimental setup:
- nail in air + water → rust on nail
- anhydrous calcium chloride (removes water) + cotton wool → no rust on nail
- oil (prevents air getting in) + boiled water (no oxygen) → no rust on nail

Prevention

Coating with paint, grease/oil, chrome plating – **barrier methods** – stops oxygen/water getting to metal.
- Sacrificial metals – galvanising (zinc) or another more reactive metal.

Iron reacts with dilute sulphuric acid in absence of oxygen → iron (II) sulphate + hydrogen:

$$Fe(s) + H_2SO_4(aq) \rightarrow FeSO_4(aq) + H_2(g)$$

In presence of oxygen (air) or concentrated sulphuric acid → iron (III) sulphate (oxidation).

Alcohols

Contain an OH group in the molecule.
Chemical family – homologous series – each substance differs from the next by a CH_2 unit – all react in similar way.

General formula: $C_nH_{2n+1}OH$
e.g. n = 1 CH_3OH methanol, n = 2 C_2H_5OH ethanol

Structure:

```
        H                    H  H
        |                    |  |
    H – C – O – H        H – C – C – O – H
        |                    |  |
        H                    H  H
```

Preparation

By fermentation – to make beers, wines and spirits – action of yeast contains enzyme zymase on glucose solution at 33°C (anaerobic respiration):

$$C_6H_{12}O_6(aq) \xrightarrow{yeast} 2C_2H_5OH(aq) + 2CO_2(g)$$

glucose   ethanol   carbon dioxide

High temperature kills yeast and denatures the enzyme.
Passing steam and ethene under pressure over a catalyst:

```
  H       H                   H  H
   \     /                    |  |
    C = C    + H2O  →   H – C – C – O – H
   /     \                    |  |
  H       H                   H  H
```

Properties of alcohols

Good fuel

Colourless liquids which mix with water.
Burn in air → carbon dioxide and water:
$$2CH_3OH(l) + 3O_2(g) \rightarrow 2CO_2(g) + 4H_2O(g) \quad \Delta H = negative$$

React with sodium metal → salt and hydrogen:
$$2C_2H_5OH(l) + 2Na(s) \rightarrow 2C_2H_5O^-Na^+(g) + H_2(g)$$

```
    H  H                          H  H
    |  |                          |  |
2 H–C– C –O–H + 2Na  →    2 H– C – C – O⁻ Na⁺ + H2
    |  |                          |  |
    H  H                          H  H
```

(cf. reaction water + sodium → 'salt' + hydrogen)
$$(2H_2O(l) + 2Na(s) \rightarrow 2NaOH(aq) + H_2(g))$$

React with organic acids $\xrightleftharpoons[H^+]{\text{conc. } H_2SO_4 \text{ catalyst}}$ esters + water (reversible reaction):

$$CH_3OH(l) + CH_3COOH(l) \rightleftharpoons CH_3COOCH_3(l) + H_2O(l)$$
methanol   ethanoic acid   methylethanoate   water

> –oate = from acid.
> –yl = from alcohol.

Ester – sweet fruity smell – flavouring in food.

Oxidised by air/acidified potassium manganate solution [O] → carboxylic acids (organic acids):

$$C_2H_5OH(l) + 2[O] \rightarrow CH_3COOH(l) + H_2O(l)$$

e.g. air → wine → ethanoic acid (tastes sour).

Carboxylic acids (organic acids) – contain COOH group – partly ionised in solution – weak acids – pH 3.

Reactions similar to hydrochloric acid/sulphuric acid.

methanoic acid   ethanoic acid

Preparation

Oxidation of alcohols:

e.g. ethanol + 2[O] → ethanoic acid + water

> N.B. similarities with HCl, H_2SO_4.

Reactions

Alkali → salt + water:

methanoic acid + sodium hydroxide → sodium methanoate + water

$$H-C(=O)-O-H + NaOH \rightarrow H-C(=O)-O^- Na^+ + H_2O$$

ethanoic acid + sodium hydroxide → sodium ethanoate + water

$$\begin{array}{c} H \quad O \\ | \quad \| \\ H-C-C \\ | \quad \backslash \\ H \quad O-H \end{array} + NaOH \rightarrow \begin{array}{c} H \quad O \\ | \quad \| \\ H-C-C \\ | \quad \backslash \\ H \quad O^-Na^+ \end{array} + H_2O$$

Alcohols → esters (see alcohols).

Solubility

Number of grams of substance dissolved in 100 grams of water (solvent) → saturated solution → at given temperature.

- **Solubility of solids increases with temperature.**
- **Solubility of all gases decreases with temperature.**
- **Increased pressure** → solubility of gas increases (e.g. fizzy drinks).

Measuring solubility at different temperature — solubility curves — comparisons of solubility:

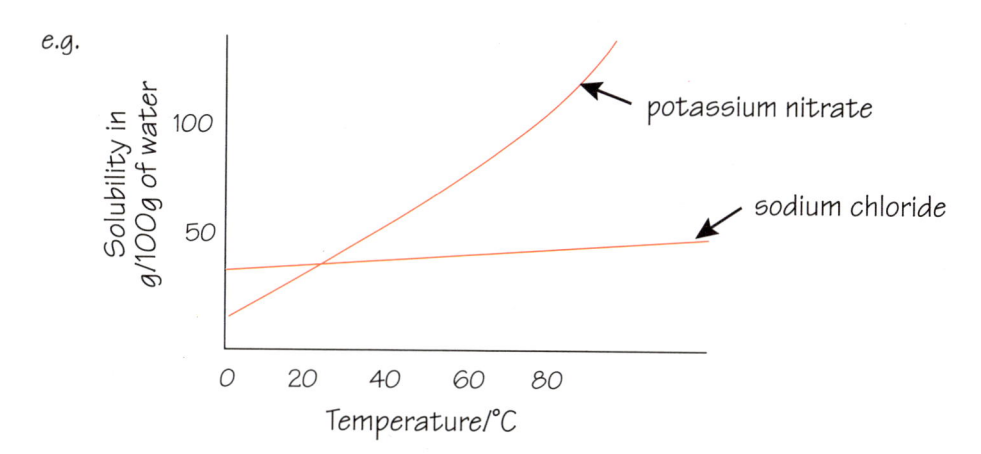

e.g.

[Graph: Solubility in g/100g of water vs Temperature/°C, showing potassium nitrate (steep curve) and sodium chloride (nearly flat)]

From graph:
- potassium nitrate more soluble than sodium chloride at all temperatures > 20°C
- solubility of potassium nitrate in hot water greater than cold
- solubility of sodium chloride hardly changes.

Cooling a saturated solution → less solid dissolves → crystallisation occurs → solid forms → settles:

e.g.

[Graph: Solubility in g/100g of water vs Temperature/°C, with dashed lines at 50°C (75 g) and 80°C (125 g)]

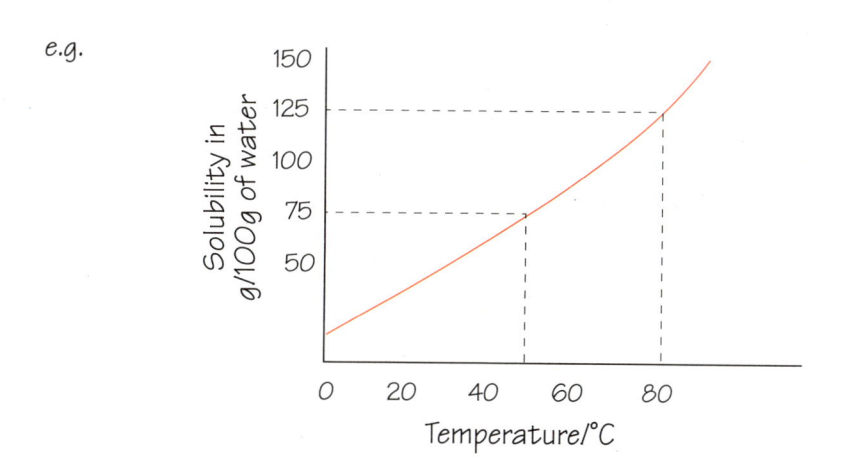

Solution cooled from 80°C to 50°C (125 − 75) g of crystals form, i.e. 50 g.

Water

Good solvent – dissolves compounds (solute) → solution.

Hard and soft water

Water from different rocks → dissolves minerals → hard or soft water:
- **hard water** – dissolved calcium and magnesium compounds – high concentrations → very hard water
- **soft water** – little or no dissolved calcium or magnesium compounds.

Two types of hardness
Permanent hardness – removed by:
- **distillation** → very pure water – expensive
- **washing soda (sodium carbonate)** → insoluble calcium carbonate → precipitates → calcium/magnesium salts removed → soft impure water – soap lathers easily

$$Na_2CO_3(s) + CaSO_4(aq) \rightarrow CaCO_3(s) + Na_2SO_4(aq)$$
washing soda   hardness   calcium carbonate

- ion exchange resin → removes **calcium/magnesium ions** → replaces with **hydrogen** or **sodium ions** → soft impure water – soap lathers easily.

hard water (MgSO$_4$)(CaSO$_4$) → ion-exchange resin → Mg^{2+}/Ca^{2+} exchanged for Na$^+$ → soft water containing Na$_2$SO$_4$(aq)

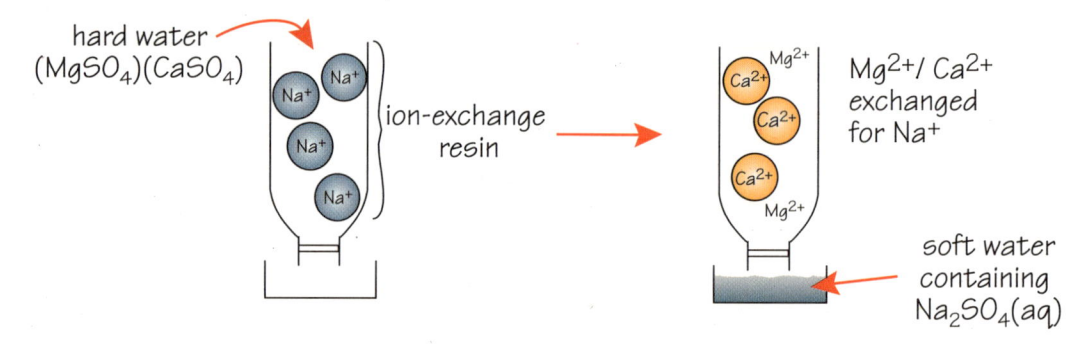

Temporary hardness:
carbon dioxide → rain → calcium carbonate rock → calcium hydrogen carbonate → hard water → boiling → decomposes calcium hydrogen carbonate → soft water and 'fur'.

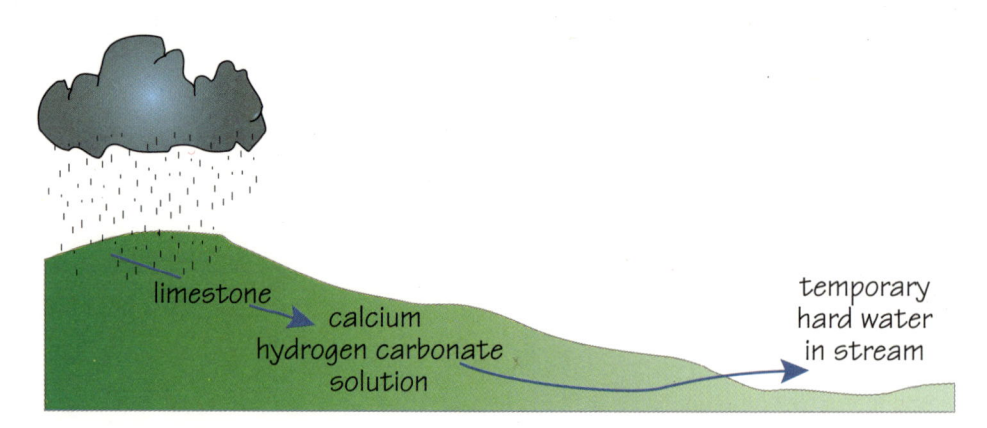

limestone → calcium hydrogen carbonate solution → temporary hard water in stream

i.e.
$$CO_2(g) + H_2O(l) + CaCO_3(s) \rightarrow Ca(HCO_3)_2(aq)$$
rain water   rock   calcium hydrogen carbonate(aq)

$$Ca(HCO_3)_2\ (aq) \xrightarrow{heat} CaCO_3(s) + CO_2(g) + H_2O(l)$$
temporary hardness　　　　　　　'fur' precipitated
(calcium hydrogencarbonate)　　(calcium carbonate)

Disadvantages of hard water

- Water + soap → scum:
  e.g.
  calcium sulphate + sodium stearate → calcium stearate + sodium sulphate
  　(hardness)　　　　(soap)　　　　　　　　　　(scum)

  Soaps clean effectively when all hardness has gone.
- Furs up kettles, boilers and pipes → dangerous.
- Uses up more electricity to heat water.

> Detergents do not form scum, they lather immediately.

> Size of hole gets smaller.

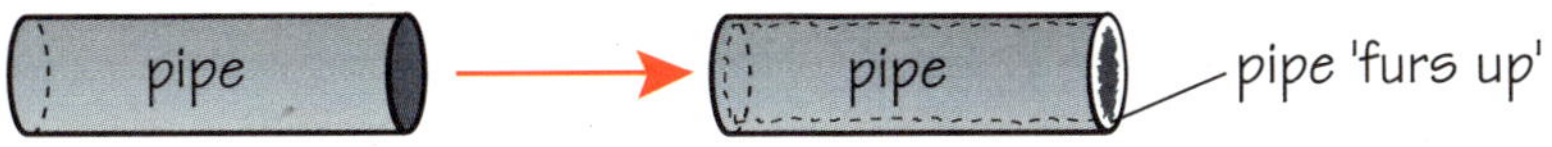

pipe → pipe — pipe 'furs up'

Advantages of hard water

Good health → strong teeth and bones, prevents heart disease.

Water purification

Water in streams/rivers → reservoir → sand beds → filtered → remove mud/most bacteria → chlorinated → kills all bacteria → safe drinking water → homes.

Water cycle

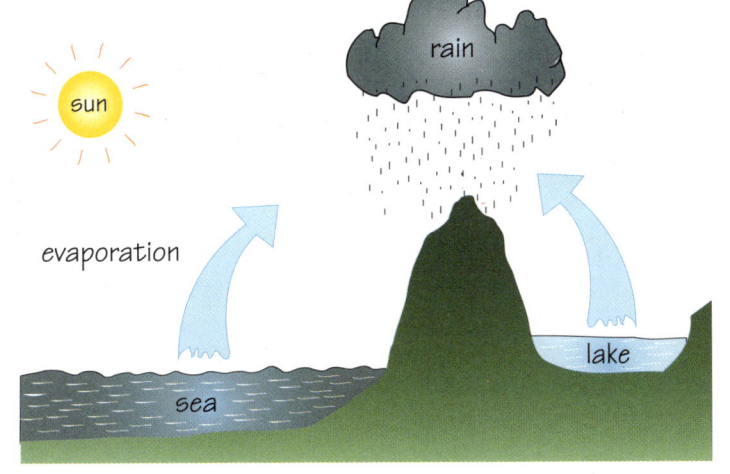

Water for homes

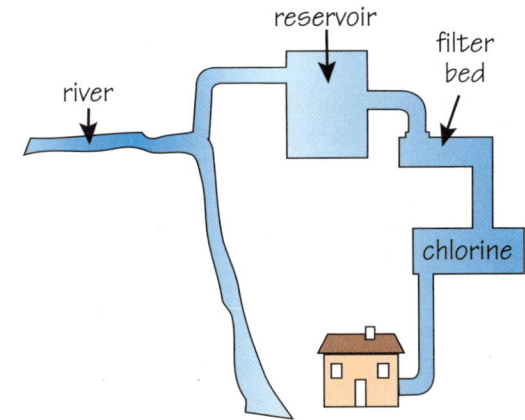

MATERIALS AND THEIR PROPERTIES

59

Chemical equations

Represent chemical reactions.

Can be shown as:
- **word equations** – reaction is written in words
- **balanced symbol equations** – reaction is written using formulae – total number of atoms of each element is same on both sides of equation
- **ionic equations** – only ions taking part in reaction are shown.

E.g. word equation   methane + oxygen → carbon dioxide + water
      balanced equation $CH_4(g) + 2O_2(g) \rightarrow CO_2(g) + 2H_2O(g)$
      ionic equation $2Cl^-(aq) \rightarrow Cl_2(g) + 2e^-$
                             $Fe^{3+}(aq) + 3e^- \rightarrow Fe(s)$

Examiner's tip
You must be able to write all types of equations.

Calculations using formulas and equations

We can use formulas and equations to calculate how much of a substance is used or how much is formed in a chemical reaction. For this we use the **mole**.

- **Solids** – 1 mole – atomic or molecular mass in grams,
  e.g. sodium chloride – NaCl: Na = 23, Cl = 35.5, NaCl = 23 + 35.5 = 58.5, 1 mole of NaCl = 58.5 g.
- **Solutions** – when 1 mole of substance is dissolved and solution made up to $1dm^3$ – resulting solution is a **molar solution**,
  e.g. molar hydrochloric acid – 1 mol/dm^3 HCl contains 1 mole of HCl per dm^3 of solution. A solution containing 0.1 mol/dm^3 HCl, contains 0.1 moles of HCl per dm^3.
  The number of moles in a solution = $\dfrac{\text{mass in grams} \times \text{volume}}{\text{molecular mass} \times 1000}$ or $\dfrac{\text{molarity} \times \text{volume}}{1000}$
- **Gases** – number of moles of gas at room temperature = $\dfrac{\text{volume of gas (cm}^3\text{)}}{24\,000}$

Examiner's tip
Write a formula – gain a mark.

Never learn numbers for calculation.

Example of calculation

In the reaction $CH_4(g) + 2O_2(g) \rightarrow CO_2(g) + 2H_2O(g)$
calculate the mass of carbon dioxide produced from 4 g of methane.

(A_r C = 12, H = 1, O = 16)

- Calculate the molecular masses – CH_4 = 12 + 4 × 1 = 16, CO_2 = 12 + 2 × 16 = 44.
- From the equation: 1 mole of methane (CH_4) produces 1 mole of carbon dioxide (CO_2).
- So 16 g of methane produces 44 g of carbon dioxide.
- Therefore 4 g of methane produces 11 g of carbon dioxide.

Finding a formula from given information

Follow these simple steps:

e.g. a gas contains 27.3 g of carbon and 72.7 g of oxygen; find its formula.

	C	O
Mass or percentage	27.3g	72.7g
Divide by atomic mass	$\frac{27.3}{12}$	$\frac{72.7}{16}$
	= 2.28	= 4.54
Divide by lowest number (to find ratio of atoms)	$\frac{2.28}{2.28}$	$\frac{4.54}{2.28}$
Empirical formula = CO_2	= 1	= 2

Examiner's tip: Show all stages of calculations.

Simplest ratio of atoms.

Finding the mass from given information

Follow these simple steps:

e.g. aluminium oxide is electrolysed for 24 hours using a steady current of 3000A; find amounts of aluminium and oxygen formed (Al = 27g and 96,000C needed to deposit ion with charge 1+).

- Balanced equation at cathode
  $Al^{3+} + 3e^- \rightarrow Al$.
- Charge passed Q = I x t (I current in amps and t time in **seconds**)
  = 3000 x 24 x 60 x 60 = 2.6×10^8 C.
- From equation: 3 moles of electrons makes 1 mole Al (27 g);
  number of coulombs needed to deposit 1 mole Al = 3 x 96,000 (charge of 3+).
- Therefore:
  mole Al formed = $\frac{3000 \times 24 \times 60 \times 60}{3 \times 96,000}$
- Mass of aluminium = moles Al x 27 g (24300 g).

Rates of reactions

Reaction can be **speeded** up by using a **catalyst** or **increasing** the following:
- **concentration** of reactant
- **surface area** of a solid (smaller particles)
- **temperature**
- **pressure** (only gaseous reactions).

Particles must have enough energy (activation energy, E_a) to **collide successfully** – **number and frequency** of collisions needs to be **high** for fast reaction.

Catalysts
- **Alter** rate of reaction and specific for a given reaction,
  e.g. MnO_2, V_2O_5, Pt and Fe or Fe_2O_3.
- **Decrease activation energy barrier** – allowing **more particles** with lower energy to react – reduces time taken and energy used, therefore cost of reaction.
- **Not used up** in chemical reactions.
- **Important** for increasing rates of industrial manufacturing processes,

Examiner's tip: Never name a catalyst unless you **know** it works for that reaction.

e.g. Contact process (H_2SO_4), Haber process (NH_3).

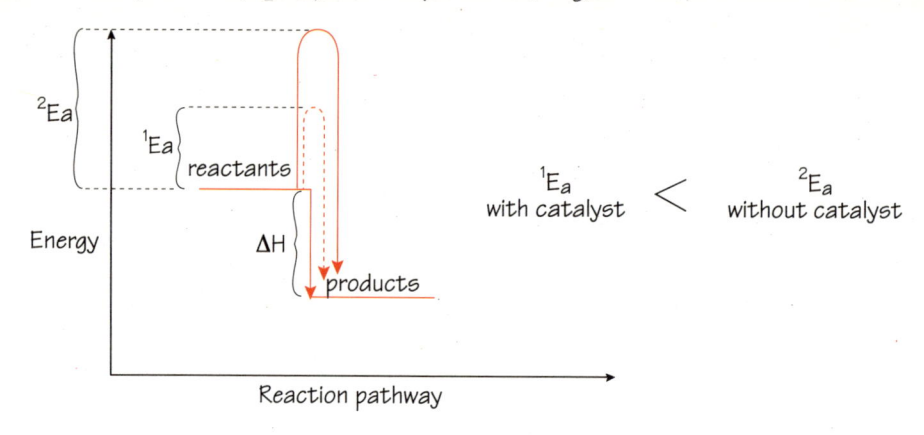

^1E_a with catalyst < ^2E_a without catalyst

ΔH **will not** change with catalyst – **only** the **rate** of reaction will alter.

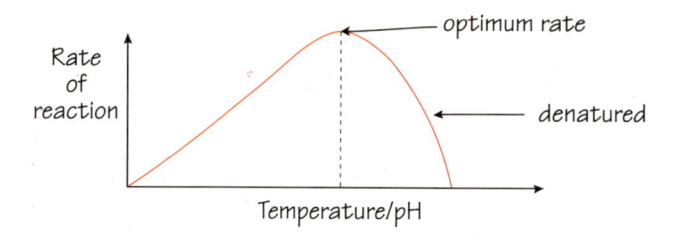

Enzymes

- Biological catalysts – **proteins**.
- Structures **denatured** (damaged) above 45°C.
- **Specific.**
- Most effective at **optimum** conditions.

- **Low** temperature **decreases** enzyme and bacterial **activity** – helps to preserve food.

Enzymes used for:
- baking (yeast) – makes **carbon dioxide** – bread rises
- wine/beers (sugar/yeast) – makes alcohol (ethanol) – **anaerobic** (**fermentation**)
- dairy industry – cheese, yoghurts (**bacteria cultures**).

Reversible reactions

See details on ammonia manufacture (page 50).

Reactant products are **constantly interchanged** but concentrations appear to be **constant**:

$$A + B \underset{}{\overset{reversible}{\rightleftharpoons}} C + D$$

- Occur in a **closed** container.
- At equilibrium – speed of both forward and backwards reactions are **equal**.
- Reaction **conditions** determine concentrations (**Le Chatelier's principle**).

Rate graphs

Comparing reaction conditions on a graph

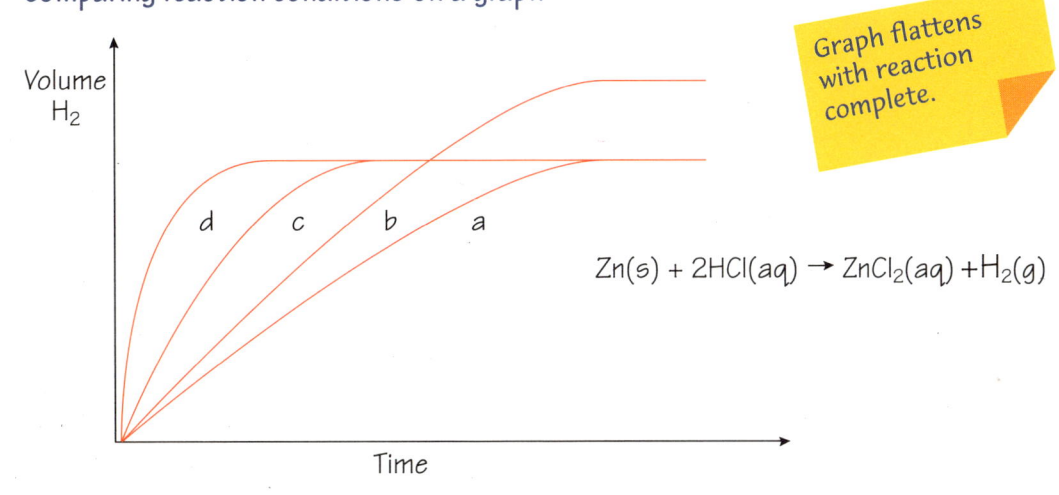

[Graph: Volume H₂ vs Time showing four curves labelled d, c, b, a from fastest/highest to slowest/lowest]

$Zn(s) + 2HCl(aq) \rightarrow ZnCl_2(aq) + H_2(g)$

Graph flattens with reaction complete.

- c – reference graph (2g Zn pieces with excess acid).
- d – same amounts – powdered zinc/catalyst added ($CuSO_4$) or higher temperature.
- a – large piece of zinc (2 g)/weaker acid.
- b – more zinc used with excess acid.

Energy changes in chemical reactions

- **Exothermic** reactions – energy **given out** – temperature **rise** – ΔH = **negative**.
- **Endothermic** reactions – energy **taken in** – temperature **drop** – ΔH = **positive**.

Energy diagram:

Exothermic reaction

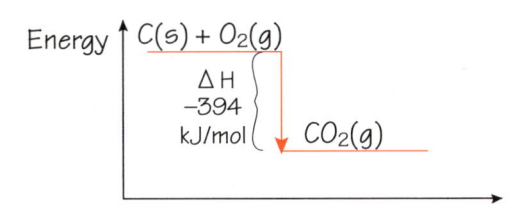

[Diagram: Energy axis; $C(s) + O_2(g)$ at higher level, dropping $\Delta H = -394$ kJ/mol to $CO_2(g)$]

e.g. **all** burning fuels

Endothermic reaction

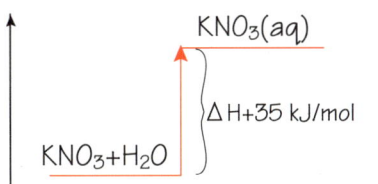

[Diagram: $KNO_3 + H_2O$ at lower level, rising ΔH +35 kJ/mol to $KNO_3(aq)$]

Potassium nitrate (aq)

Note: Most reactions are exothermic.

You must be able to draw energy diagrams.

During a chemical reaction

- Energy must be supplied to break bonds.
- Energy is released when bonds form.

Exothermic

Energy
reactants
products
Reaction pathway

Endothermic

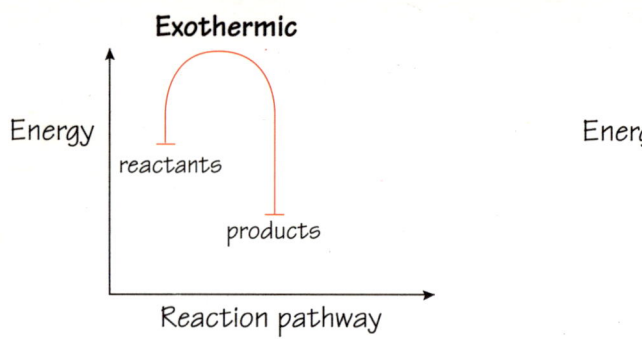

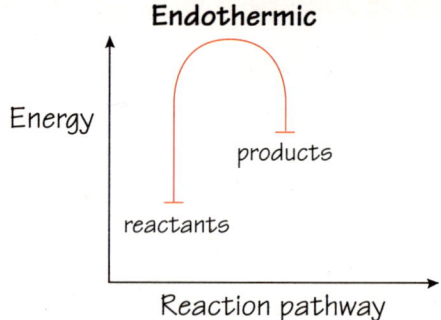

Energy
products
reactants
Reaction pathway

Calculating energy changes

Can use formulae and equations to calculate how much energy is used and how much is formed in a chemical reaction. For this we use **bond energies**.

You may not need to break every bond in reactions.

Example of a calculation:
$CH_4 + 2O_2 \rightarrow CO_2 + 2H_2O$
- Calculate the energy change – is reaction endo/exothermic? Bond energy: C–H = 413, O=O = 498, C=O = 803, O–H = 463 kJ/mol.
- Calculate total energy to break the bonds (+):
  4 C–H bonds = 4 x 413 = 1652
  2 O=O bonds = 2 x 498 = 996
  Total = 2648 kJ.
- Calculate the total energy when bonds are formed:
  2 C=O bonds = 2 x 803 = 1606
  4 O–H bonds = 4 x 463 = 1852
  Total 3458 kJ.
- Net change = + 2648 – 3458 = – 810 kJ.
- Reaction is exothermic – heat absorbed when bonds of CH_4 and O_2 broken less than heat given out when bonds of CO_2 and H_2O formed.

Examiner's tip
Don't forget the **sign** (+ or −) and **units**.

Examiner's tip
Relate 810 kJ to exothermic energy diagram.

Geological changes

3 types of rock – igneous, sedimentary and metamorphic.

- **Igneous rocks** – cooling down of molten rock (magma) → random, interlocking crystals of different minerals.
  – Slow cooling (within Earth's crust) – large crystals, easily seen – intrusive rock, e.g. granite.
  – Rapid cooling (erupted from volcanoes) – small crystals, seen under microscope – extrusive rock, e.g. basalt.

- **Sedimentary** rocks – deposition of sediments in layers followed by compression – pressure of layers above – squeezes out water – cementation of sediment particles → rock, e.g. chalk, limestone, sandstone, mudstone.

- May contain fossils – remains of plants, animals trapped between layers (often shelly) – used to identify and date rocks.

- **Metamorphic** rocks – action of heat and pressure on existing rocks, e.g. limestone to marble, mudstone to slate and schist (banded rock with interlocking crystals).

- Movement of tectonic plates → mountain building and burial of rocks deep underground – become heated and compressed → metamorphic rock.

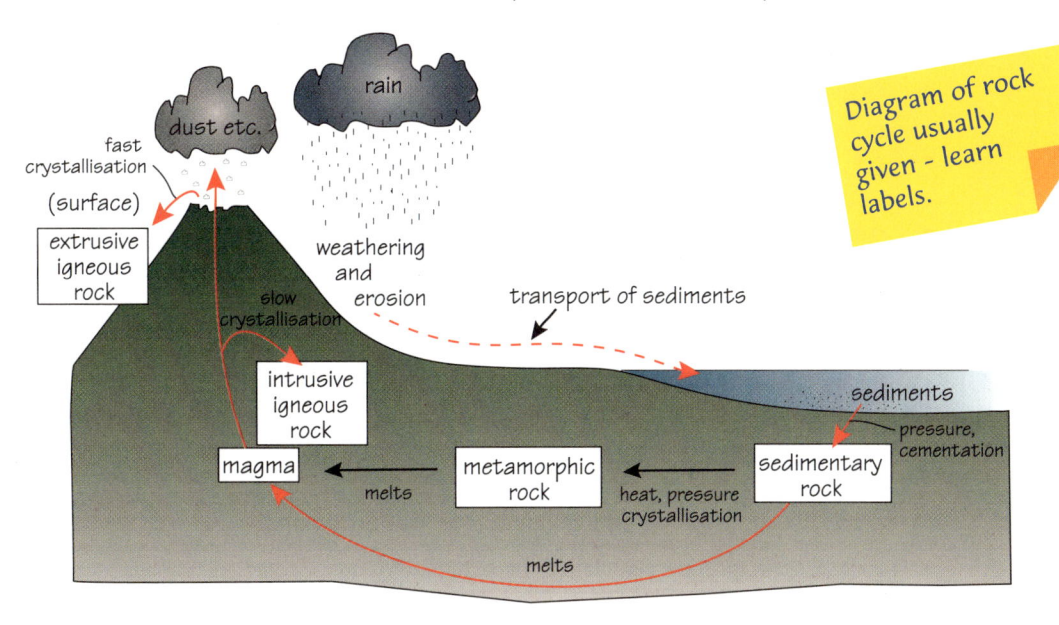

Diagram of rock cycle usually given - learn labels.

Examiner's tip
You must be able to explain how it happens.

- **Weathering** and erosion also responsible for recycling of surface rock.
- Weathering – **breakdown** of rock by water, wind, animals, plant roots, chemicals.
- Erosion – **carrying away** of rock by water, wind, gravity.

Plate tectonics

Structure of the Earth – evidence from earthquake waves:

Size of earthquake measured on the Richter scale.

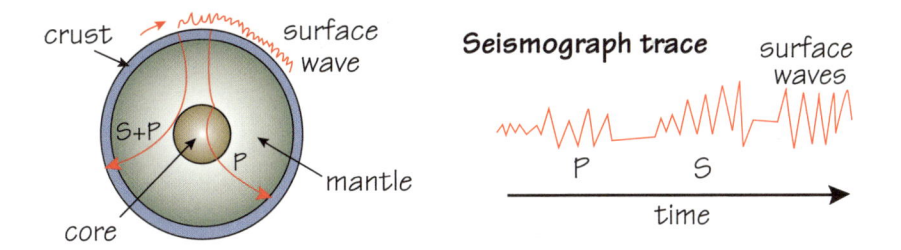

- **S and P shock waves allow structure of Earth to be worked out**
  - **fast P waves** travel through **liquids and solids**
  - **slow S waves** travel only in **solids**.

The Earth has:
- a thin **crust** (about 20 km thick)
- a **mantle** – very viscous liquid
- a dense **core** (just over half Earth's radius) made of **nickel** and **iron** – origin of Earth's magnetic field – outer core liquid, inner core solid
- **crust is less dense** than overall density of Earth – shows interior of Earth made of different and denser material.

Changes to the atmosphere

- **Volcanic activity** – first billion years of Earth's existence – released gases → original atmosphere.
- Contained carbon dioxide, methane, ammonia, water vapour → condensed → oceans (little/no oxygen present).

MATERIALS AND THEIR PROPERTIES

65

- **Plants evolved** – photosynthesis developed – changed carbon dioxide into oxygen → used in respiration – carbon locked in plants, formed fossil fuels.
- Methane and ammonia reacted with oxygen → nitrogen.
- **Living organisms** and **denitrifying** bacteria made more nitrogen.
- Oxygen led to development of **ozone layer** – filters harmful UV rays from sunlight – new organisms could evolve.
- Carbon dioxide absorbed by sea water → sediments of carbonate rocks and soluble hydrogencarbonates (mainly calcium and magnesium).
- Composition of atmosphere maintained by **carbon cycle** – animals, plants and microorganisms.

Examiner's tip
Be able to describe what happens if...

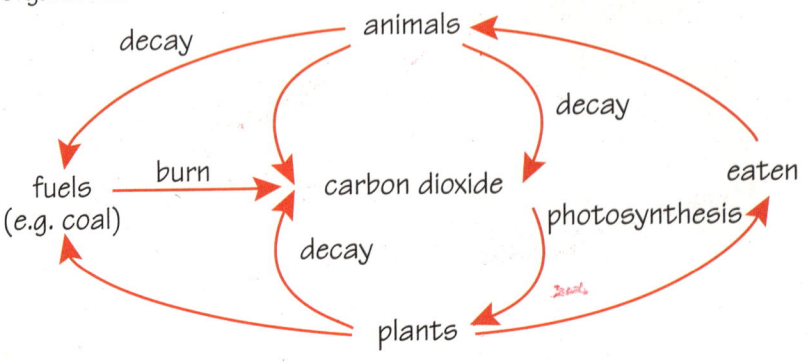

Crude oil (petroleum) and hydrocarbons

- Crude oil (petroleum) – formed in several steps over **millions of years**: sea creatures die → sink to sea bed → covered by rock → heat and pressure causes them to decay (anaerobic) → oil and gas.
- Crude oil can be separated into **fractions** according to their **boiling points** by **fractional distillation**.

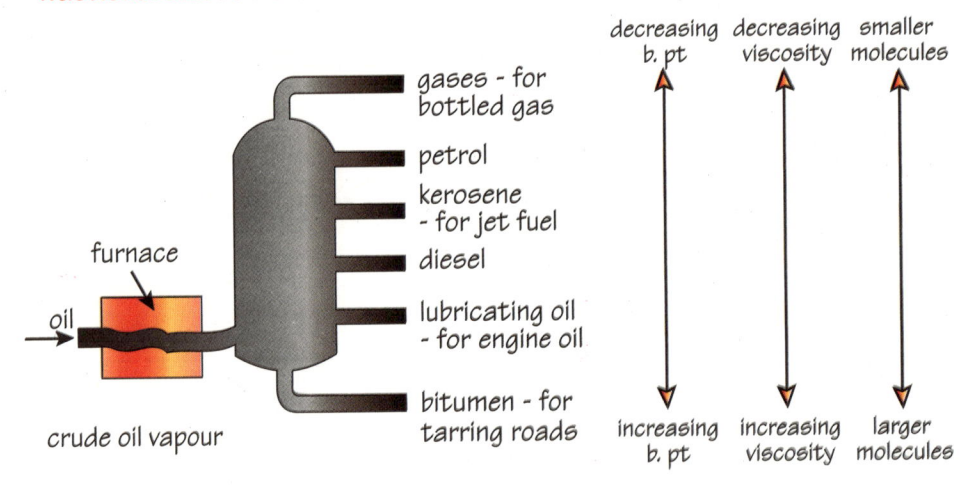

Examiner's tip
Key word **only**.

- Crude oil contains **hydrocarbons**.
- Hydrocarbons contain **only hydrogen** and **carbon**.
- They **burn** in a **good** supply of air (oxygen) to form **carbon dioxide** and **water**.
- In a **limited** supply of air → **carbon monoxide** formed (**very poisonous**).

Saturated hydrocarbons → alkanes

- Molecules in which carbon atoms are linked by single **C–C covalent bonds**, e.g. methane (g)   ethane (g)   propane (g)

CH_4 C_2H_6 C_3H_8

Unsaturated hydrocarbons → alkenes

- Molecules in which carbon atoms are linked by at least one **double C=C bonds**,
  e.g.   ethene (g)   propene (g)

  $$H_2C=CH_2 \qquad H_3C-CH=CH_2$$

- React by breaking double bond and other atoms added on – **addition reactions** – bonds become single,
  e.g.

  $$H_2C=CH_2 + Br-Br \text{ (red/orange)} \rightarrow CH_2Br-CH_2Br \text{ (colourless)}$$

  Brown bromine water decolourised by double \\C=C/ bonds

  No colour change with single -C-C- bonds

  Br_2 – used to test for C=C bonds.

Cracking

Process in which large hydrocarbon molecules are **broken down** into **smaller, more useful molecules**. High temperature, high pressure and catalyst needed.
E.g.
Word equation   decane → octane   + ethene
                                     for petrol   (to make polyethene)
Chemical equation $C_{10}H_{22}$ → C_8H_{18} + C_2H_4

Examiner's tip
Carbons and hydrogens equal on both sides.

Macromolecules (polymers)

- Very large molecules which have very useful properties.

  Two types:

- **addition polymers** – **large number of small molecules (monomers) join together → polymer → process called polymerisation**

  $$n\, C_2H_4 \rightarrow \cdots(-CH_2-CH_2-)_n \cdots \text{ poly(ethene)}$$

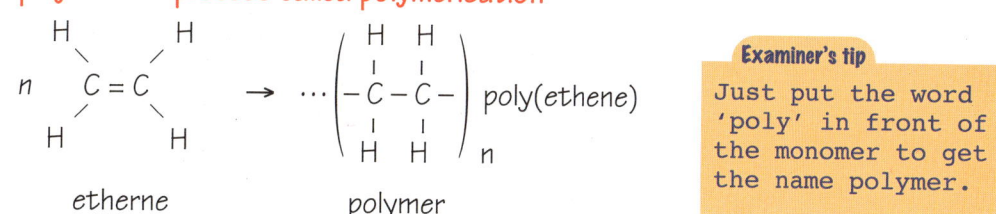

  ethene monomer   polymer ($n > 50$)

  Examiner's tip
  Just put the word 'poly' in front of the monomer to get the name polymer.

- **condensation polymers** – **monomers join together to form a large chain and a small molecule**, e.g. water, **is given out**

  $$n\left(H_2N-\square-NH_2 \;+\; HOOC-\square-COOH \right) \rightarrow \left(-HN-\square-NH-CO-\square-CO-\right)_n + nH_2O$$

  monomer 1   monomer 2   polymer + nH_2O

- **Synthetic** polymers, e.g. nylon, polyester.
- **Natural** polymers, e.g. starch (**monomer – glucose**), proteins (**monomers – amino acids**).

67

Questions

1. In an experiment it was found that 1.12 g of iron reacted with 2.13 g of chlorine. Calculate the formula of the compound formed (relative atomic mass: Fe = 56, Cl = 35.5).

   _____
   _____
   _____
   _____

2. A molten electrolyte contains sodium ions, Na^+ and chloride ions, Cl^-.

   (a) Explain why the electrolyte conducts electricity.

   _____
   _____

   (b) Chloride ions, Cl^-, react at the anode.

   The equation for the reaction is: _____

   This is an example of oxidation. Explain why.

   _____

3. A hydrocarbon, propane (C_3H_8), was burned in a plentiful supply of air (oxygen).

   (a) Write a word and a balanced chemical equation for the reaction.

   word equation _____

   chemical equation_____

   (b) A hydrocarbon is a substance which contains_____ and _____ only.

   (c) Crude oil can be_____ into_____ by the process of

   _____

4. The amount of carbon dioxide and oxygen in the atmosphere stays roughly constant.

   Green plants take in_____ and change it into food and_____.

   This process is called_____. When fossil fuels are burned_____ is used up.

5. Ammonia is formed from hydrogen and nitrogen.

   $$N_2(g) + 3H_2(g) \rightleftharpoons 2NH_3(g) \quad \Delta H = -92 \text{ kJ/mol}$$

   Explain how the equilibrium could be shifted to the left (increasing reactants).

   _____
   _____

Answers

Classifying materials

1 (a) 7, 3, (2, 1)
   7, 3, 4, 2 (2)
   6, 6 (2, 4)
   7, 6 (2, 4)
   20, 10 (2, 8)
   16, 16, (2, 8, 8)
(b) Li^+, Ne and S^{2-}

2

3

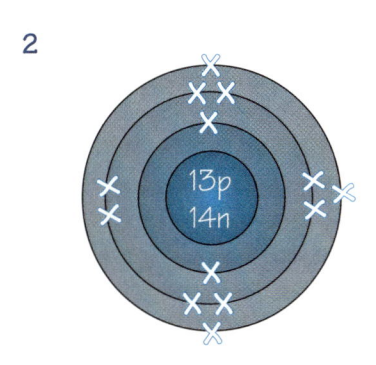

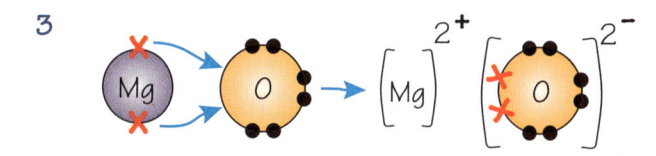

4 Protons, electrons

5 (a) A
  (b) C
  (c) B

Patterns of behaviour

1 (a) A/B/C/D (b) E (c) D (d) $2Ca + O_2 \rightarrow 2CaO$ 2 (a) Group 1, alkali metals, under oil, reacts, water (b) floats, moves on surface, fumes, cloudy solution 3 Haber process, ammonia 4 Noble gases, react, 8 (O) 5 Group 7, halogens $Cl_2 + 2Br^- \rightarrow 2Cl^- + Br_2$, displacement reaction 6 Hard, high density, catalysts 7 (a) bromine (b) sodium chloride (c) silver bromide

Changing materials

1 mol Fe = 1.12/56 = 0.02 mol Cl = 2.13/35.5 = 0.06 Ratio Fe : Cl = 1 : 3, formula $FeCl_3$ 2 (a) Ions are free to move about. (b) $2Cl^- \rightarrow Cl_2 + 2e^-$ or $2Cl^- - 2e^- \rightarrow Cl_2$ or $Cl^- \rightarrow Cl + e$ electrons are being lost. 3 (a) propane + oxygen $\rightarrow$ carbon dioxide + water $C_3H_8 + 5O_2 \rightarrow 3CO_2 + 4H_2O$ (b) Hydrogen, carbon (c) Separated, fractions, fractional distillation 4 Carbon dioxide, oxygen, photosynthesis, oxygen 5 Any of following: increasing the temperature, decreasing the pressure, removing the reactants, adding more ammonia

Electricity and magnetism

Electrostatics

- **Static electricity** – electric charges *stationary*.
- **Charges** – *positive* (+) or *negative* (−).
- **Insulators** – substances in which *electricity cannot flow*, e.g. plastics.
- **Conductors** – substances in which *electricity can flow*, e.g. metals.
- **Electron transfer** – two insulators rubbed together.
- **Insulator + electrons** → *negative charge* (−).
- **Insulator − electrons** → *positive charge* (+).

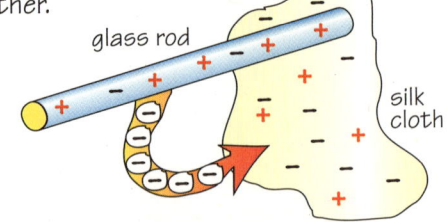

Charged objects

- **Like charges repel** + and + or − and −.
- **Unlike charges attract** + and −.
- **Charged objects attract uncharged** objects.

Unlike magnetic poles also attract.

Applications

Electrostatic filters – used to clean smoky chimneys.
Aircraft fuel lines – earthed to avoid sparks/fire.

Electrolysis

- **Ionic compounds**, e.g. sodium chloride NaCl *conduct electricity* when molten or dissolved in water.
- **Negative (−) ions flow to anode** (positive electrode).
- **Positive (+) ions flow to cathode** (negative electrode).
- **Substances deposited/released at electrodes.**
- **Amount of substance deposited/released greater when**
  – the size of the current greater
  – the time for which the current flows greater.

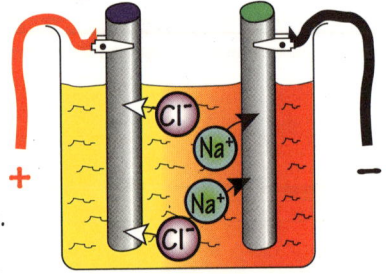

Examiner's tip
You need to be able to describe dangers and uses.

Current electricity

Resistance

- **Current electricity** – (negative) electric charges *move*.
- **Resistance** – anything that *hinders movement*.
- **Resistance of conductor greater** – conductor *longer or thinner*
  – conductor *hotter*.
- **Resistance different** – *different materials*, e.g. copper and lead.
- Resistance = $\dfrac{\text{voltage}}{\text{current}}$
- **Units** – *ohms* (Ω).
- **Ohm's law** – voltage proportional to current.

thin or long = high resistance
fat or short = low resistance

Current – voltage graphs for different components

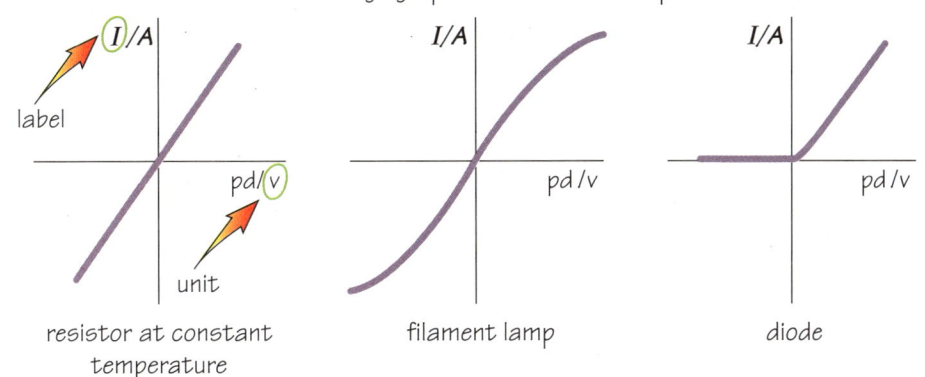

resistor at constant temperature

filament lamp

diode

Examiner's tip
Graphs should have a label and unit on each axis.

- **Ohmic conductor** – **resistance constant** (graph a) e.g. metal wire.
- **Non-ohmic conductor** – **resistance varies** (graph b) e.g. lamp filament
    - resistance thermistor decreases as temperature rises
    - resistance LDR decreases as light level rises.
- **Series resistors** $R = R_1 + R_2$
    - current same
    - potential difference (pd) divided up. 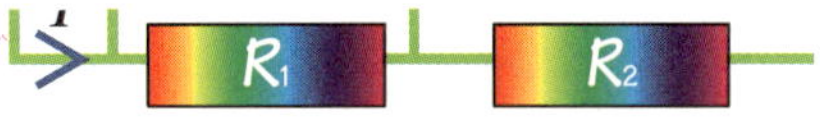
- **Parallel resistors** $\frac{1}{R} = \frac{1}{R_1} + \frac{1}{R_2}$
    - current divided $I = I_1 + I_2$
    - pd same.

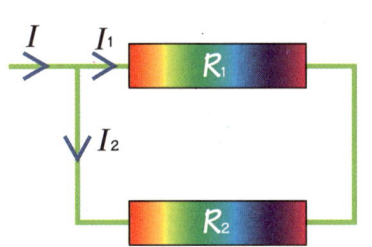

Note that 'I' is the symbol for current. 'A' stands for Amperes (Amps).

If $R_1 = R_2$,
$R = R_1/2$
$= R_2/2$

Using electricity

Energy in circuits

- **Electric current** – flow of charge.
- **Energy** – given to each electron by battery/power supply.
- **More energy** – (pd) higher.
- **1 V** – 1 J per coulomb of charge (C).
- **1 A** – current when 1 C flows/second.
- **Energy transfer** –
    $Power = pd \times current$ = energy transfer/second.
- **Units of power** – 1 W = 1 J/s.

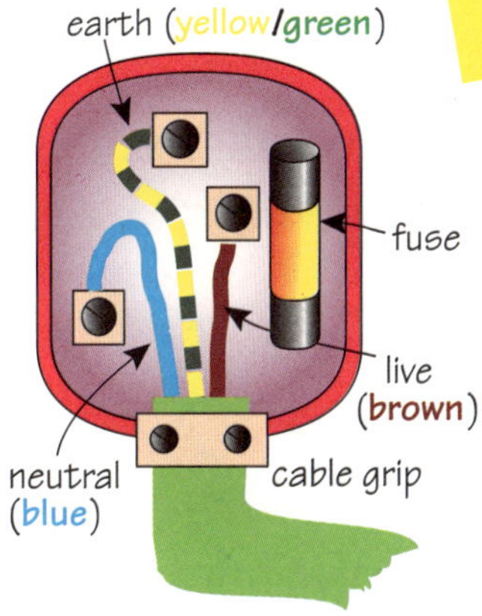

earth (yellow/green)
fuse
live (brown)
neutral (blue)
cable grip

Safety

Examiner's tip
ere is ually a estion plugs d/or fuses.

- **Fuse** – low melting-point wire.
- **Plug** – 3-pin plug needs correct fuse.
- **Fuse size** – use I = P/V where p is the power rating in Watts.
- **High current** e.g. 12 A – large fuse, 13 A.
- **Low current** e.g. 1 A – small fuse, 2 A.
- **Circuit breaker** – instead of fuse.
- **Metal** case – appliance must be earthed.
- **Plastic** case – extra protection.
    - said to be 'double insulated'.

Cost

- **Unit** – kilowatt hour (kWh).
- **Kilowatt** – 1000 watts.
- **Total cost** – number of units × cost per unit
- **Example** – 3 kW for 3 hours = 9 units
    9 units @ 6p = 54p.

Application of heating effect in a resistor

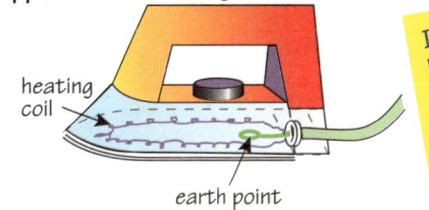

heating coil
earth point

If live wire loose large current → earth.

Electomagnetism

Magnets
- Like poles repel, unlike attract.

Electromagnets
- **Electromagnet** – coil of wire with electric current.
- **Strength** of an electromagnet **increased by**
  - placing an **iron core** in it
  - **increasing the number of turns of wire**
  - **increasing size of current** through it.
- Applications:
- **electric bell** – hammer attracted by electromagnet when current flows
- **relay** – switch closed when electromagnet activated.

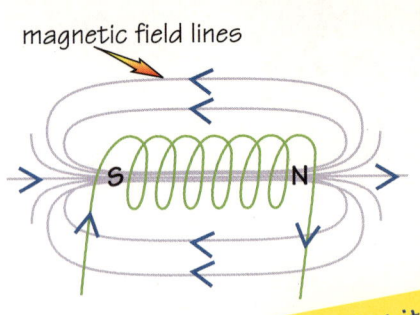

Note that it behaves like a bar magnet.

Electromagnetic forces
- **Force on wire in magnetic field.**
- **Direction of force** –
  - Fleming's **Left Hand Rule**
  - **direction** of force **reverses** if **current reverses.**
- **Size of force increases with**
  - strength of **magnetic field**
  - size of **current**
  - increased **number of turns of wire.**
- Applications:
- **motors** – force produces **rotary movement** e.g. electric drill, washing machine
- **loudspeakers** – **cone forced in and out** to produce sound waves
- **circuit breakers** – high current activates electromagnet.

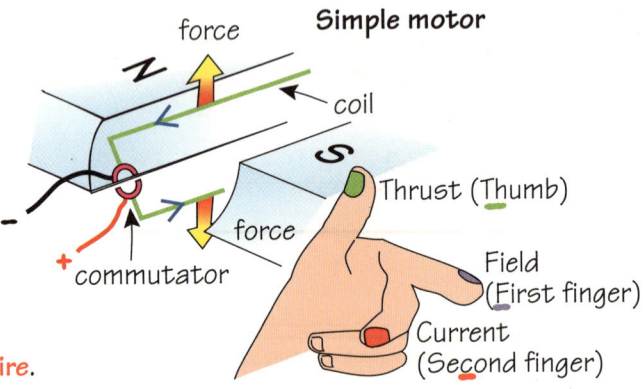

Simple motor — Thrust (Thumb), Field (First finger), Current (Second finger)

Examiner's tip: Examiners often set questions on applications to show an understanding of the principles.

Electromagnetic induction
- **Magnet** → coil of wire – current induced.
- **Coil of wire** → magnet – current induced.
- **No movement** – no current.
- Applications:
- **generator/dynamo** – produces electricity
- **transformers** (see below) – change **size** of a **voltage**.

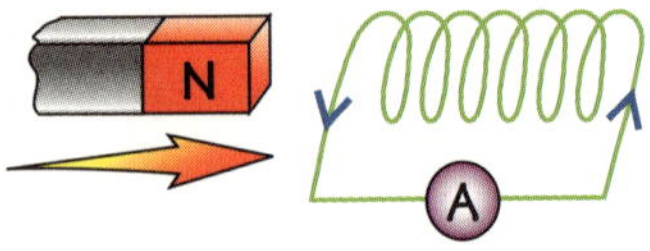

Alternating current
- Direct current (dc) – electrons move in one direction.
- **Batteries produce dc.**
- **Alternating current** (ac) – electrons change direction.
- **Power stations produce ac.**

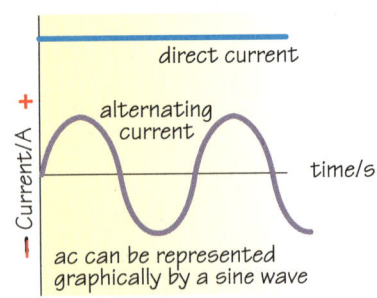

ac can be represented graphically by a sine wave

Use the right hand rule to find the direction of the current in a generator.

Transformers
- **High current** – a lot of **heat.**
- **High voltage** – avoid heat loss.
- **Power stations** – produce electricity at **high voltage.**
- **Transformers** – step down (or up) voltages
  - work on ac not dc.
- **Electricity at home** – 240 V ac (in UK).

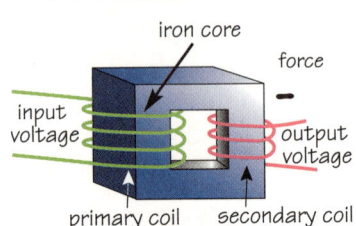

secondary pd = primary pd × no. secondary turns/no. primary turns

Questions

1. In terms of charge transfer, describe what happens when you rub a glass rod with a silk cloth. _____
_____

2. In this circuit, the two lamps are identical.

    (a) What is the pd across each lamp? _____ V

    (b) If the current flow in the main part of the circuit is 3.0 A, calculate the resistance of each lamp filament.

    _____
    _____
    _____

3. An electric kettle is rated at 1.5 kW.

    (a) Assuming that the domestic voltage supply is 250 V, what is the correct-sized fuse for the plug? (Choose from the following sizes: 1 A, 2 A, 3 A, 5 A, 10 A, 13 A.) _____
    _____

    (b) A unit of electricity costs 6p. How much does it cost to operate the kettle each day for a week, 20 minutes a day? _____
    _____

4. (a) What is meant by a step-up transformer? _____
    _____

    (b) The primary coil of a transformer has 100 turns. A pd of 2.0 V is applied across it. If an output voltage of 7.0 V is needed, how many turns of wire should the secondary coil have? _____
    _____
    _____

PHYSICAL PROCESSES

PHYSICAL PROCESSES

Forces and motion

Representing motion

Distance - time graphs

- Speed = distance/time
- Units – m/s (ms^{-1}).
- Graph a – stationary body.
- Graphs b and c – steady speed.
- Gradient → speed.
- b faster than c.

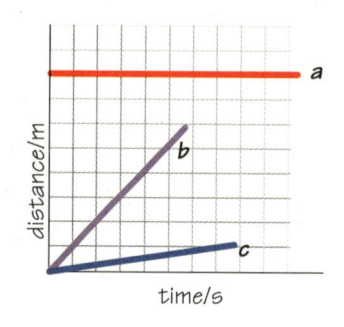

Examiner's tip
Examiners usually set questions on drawing or interpreting graphs.

Velocity - time graphs

- Acceleration = change in velocity/time taken
- Units – m/s^2 (ms^{-2}).
- Graph a – constant velocity.
- Graphs b and c – constant acceleration.
- Gradient → acceleration.
- b greater acceleration than c.

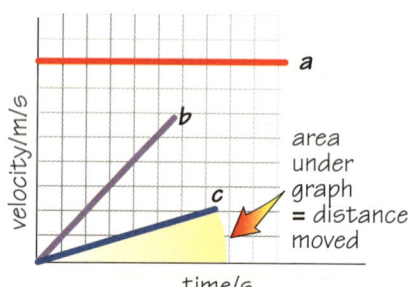

area under graph = distance moved

Force - extension graphs

- Linear part – F ∝ e (Hooke's Law).
- OA – elastic region
- AB – plastic region
- B – yield point; wire stretches with little load
- C – breaking point.

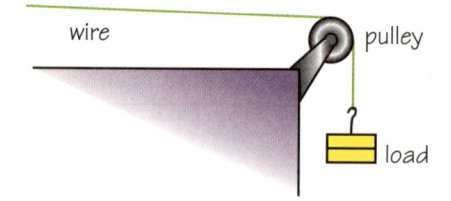

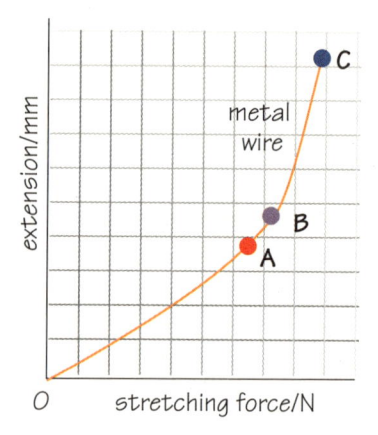

Balanced forces

- Weight, W – downwards on table.
- Force, R – upwards on book.
- R = W – forces balance.
    – book stationary.

- Thrust, T – car pushed through air.
- Force, R – air drag on car.
- R = T – forces balance
    – car constant speed.

- W greater than R → book falls!

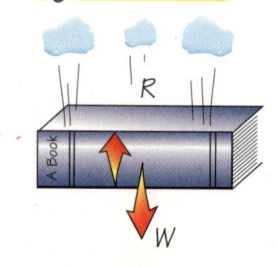

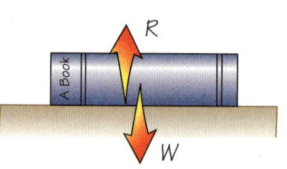

Other (frictional) forces also act on the car

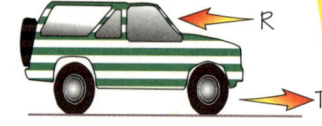

- T greater than R → car accelerates!
- Forces unbalanced.
- Unbalanced forces – change in motion.
- Force = mass × acceleration
- Units – Newtons (N).
- 1 N – 1 kg m/s^2.

Friction

- **Friction acts**
  - between two **surfaces that move**
  - when **body moves through gas or liquid.**
- **Friction** – **opposes motion**
  - causes **heating/wear**, e.g. car engine
  - **needed** for moving and stopping.

> **Examiner's tip**
> You need to be able to state or describe both advantages and disadvantages.

Road safety

- **Stopping distance depends on**
  - driver **reaction time**
  - **braking distance.**
- **Braking distance depends on**
  - **speed** – **brakes**
  - **tyres** – **road surface.**

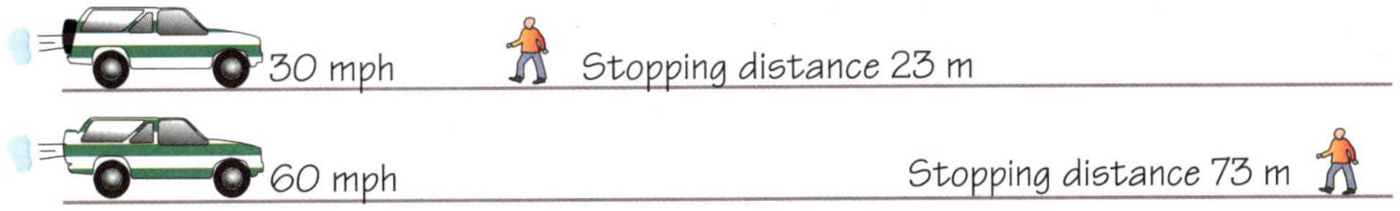

30 mph — Stopping distance 23 m
60 mph — Stopping distance 73 m

Free fall

- **Weight** → **acceleration.**
- **Air drag, R** – **increases** with speed.
- **R = W** → **terminal velocity.**
- **Terminal velocity** – **constant**
  - **zero acceleration**
  - about **120 mph** in air.

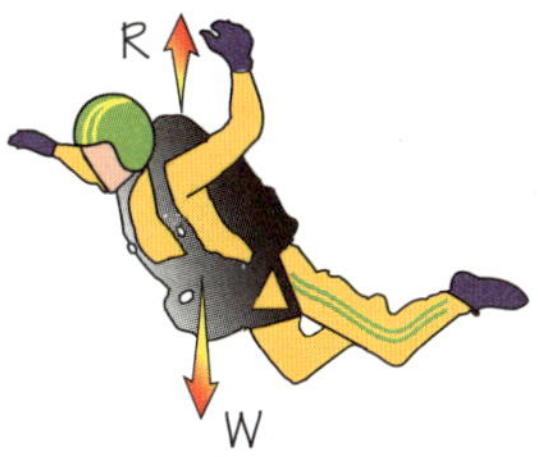

Turning forces

- **Weight** – **windmill turns.**
- **Turning effect greater if**
  - **weight** (or force) **greater**
  - **distance** to pivot is **greater.**
- **Turning effect** = **force x perpendicular distance to pivot**
- **Moment** – another name for **turning effect.**

- **Centre of mass** – where body **balances**
- **RH force/s** – turn beam ↷
- **LH force/s** – turn beam ↶
- **balance** – ↶ moments = ↷ moments

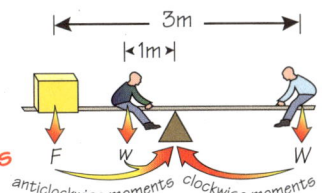

$F \times 1.5 + w \times 1 = W \times 1.5$

anticlockwise moments / clockwise moments

- **Stable** – **weight line inside base.**
- **Unstable** – **falls** if pushed
  - **weight line outside base.**
- **Neutral** – **centre of mass stays same height.**

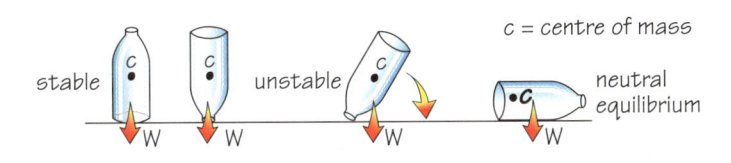

stable / unstable / neutral equilibrium
c = centre of mass

> Words clockwise and anticlockwise don't need to appear if symbols ↶ and ↷ do.

> Stability increases if centre of mass is nearer ground, e.g. sports car.

PHYSICAL PROCESSES

Momentum

- Momentum = mass x velocity
- Units – kg m/s.
- Collision/explosion – –ve force = +ve force → momentum change.
- Conservation – momentum before = momentum after
  – KE usually less after collision → heat/sound.

Examiner's tip
Remember to quote correct units in a calculation.

Planetary orbits are not perfectly circular; they are elliptical.

Circular motion

Stability

- Circular path – direction changes → velocity changes → acceleration.
- Centripetal force – acts on body since $f = m \times a$
  – acts towards centre.
- Centripetal force greater if
  – mass of body greater
  – speed of body greater
  – radius of circle smaller.
- Examples – planetary motion/motion of satellites
  – car rounding a bend.

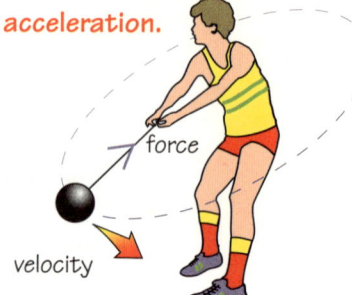

Pressure

Solids

- Pressure = force/area
- Units – N/m^2.
- $1 N/m^2$ = 1 pascal (Pa).
- Stiletto heel – small area.
- Small area → high pressure.
- Snow skis – large area.
- Large area → low pressure.

Example of high pressure

Example of low pressure

Liquids

- Pressure = $d \times h \times g$
- d – density   density = mass/volume
- h – depth.
- g – gravitational field strength (10 N/kg).
- Pressure – equal in all directions.

Example:
- hydraulic system – e.g. car jack, car brakes
- master piston A – transmits pressure
- brake piston B – pressed by liquid – has larger area
- P = F/A → force α area
- force exerted – larger
  – magnified by ratio of area B/area A.

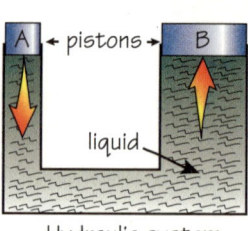

A dam is thicker at its base

Hydraulic system

This is the important bit to remember in calculations.

Gases

- Volume of gas – decreases when pressure increases.
- Temperature – constant.
- Mathematically – V α 1/P V Boyle's Law
  – $P_1V_1 = P_2V_2$.
- Example – bicycle pump – press on piston
  – volume of air decreases.

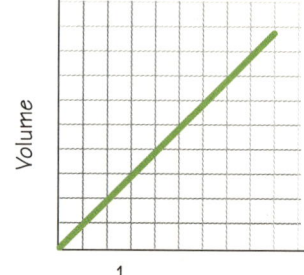

Examiner's tip
You should be able to explain gas pressure in terms of particles colliding with container walls.

Questions

1. A lorry starts from rest. A velocity – time graph of its motion is drawn for the first 30 seconds.

    (a) Describe its motion _____

    _____

    (b) Calculate

    i) its acceleration _____

    _____

    ii) the distance moved _____

    _____

2. The mass of a sports car is 1200 kg. The engine provides a thrust of 6500 N. Over a measured course, the average air drag is found to be 850 N.

    (a) What acceleration is produced? _____

    _____

    (b) What does the total stopping distance depend upon? _____

    _____

3. A uniform beam of length 2.5 m is used to weigh sacks of flour. A weight of 120 N has to be placed at point X for it to balance.
    X is 0.5 m from the pivot.
    What is the weight of the flour?
    _____

    _____

4. Bus A of mass 5000 kg is travelling east at 10 m/s. At the same time, bus B of mass 3000 kg is travelling in the same direction at 5 m/s.
    When they collide A and B move together as one. At what speed will they continue to move?

    _____

    _____

    _____

5. In a car brake system, the brake pedal pushes on a master piston of area 0.1 m² with a force of 150 N. If the brake piston is of area 0.4 m², what force is exerted on the wheels to stop them?

    _____

    _____

Waves

- **Waves transfer energy** not matter.

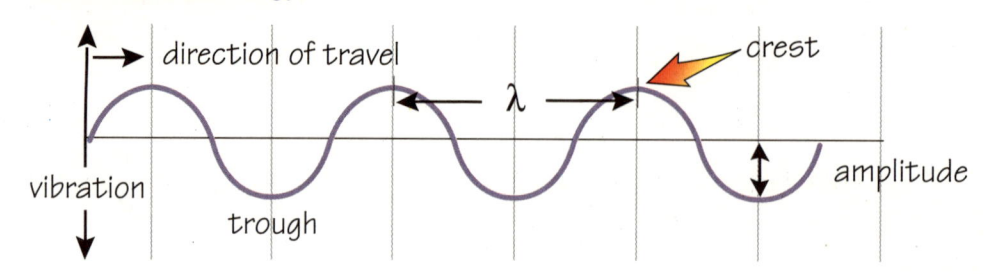

(diagram: transverse wave showing direction of travel, vibration, crest, trough, wavelength λ, amplitude)

Transverse waves

- **Examples** – water, light, radio.
- **Vibration** – 90° to direction of travel.
- **Wavelength (λ)** – from one crest to the next.
- **Frequency** – number of waves per second; 1 Hz = 1 wave/sec.
- **Electromagnetic waves** e.g. light can travel in a vacuum.

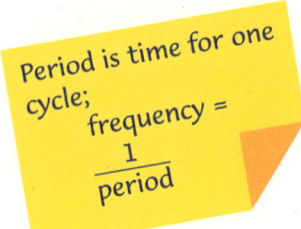

> Period is time for one cycle;
> frequency = $\dfrac{1}{\text{period}}$

Longitudinal waves

- **Examples** – sound, slinky spring as diagram below.
- **Vibration** – same direction as travel.
- **Wavelength** – from one compression to the next.
- **Sound travels in solids, liquids, gases but not a vacuum.**

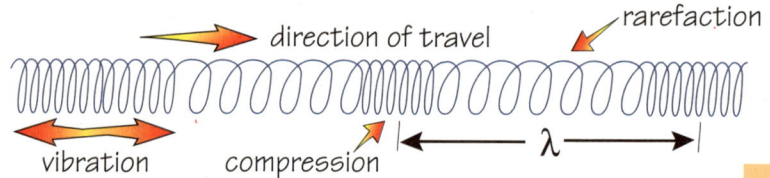

(diagram: longitudinal wave on slinky showing direction of travel, vibration, compression, rarefaction, wavelength λ)

- **Wavespeed** = wavelength × frequency $v = \lambda \times f$

> **Examiner's tip**
> Often, questions on sound waves will show them looking like transverse waves.

Properties of waves

Reflection

- Angle i = angle r for all waves.
- Mirror image – virtual
    - same size
    - upright
    - OM = MI.

> **Examiner's tip**
> Remember arrows on diagram show direction of the light.

> A quick way to draw this accurately:-
> 1) draw object + 2 incident rays
> 2) since OM = MI, draw in image
> 3) draw dotted lines joining incident rays to image
> 4) extend dotted lines as rays on LH side of mirror.

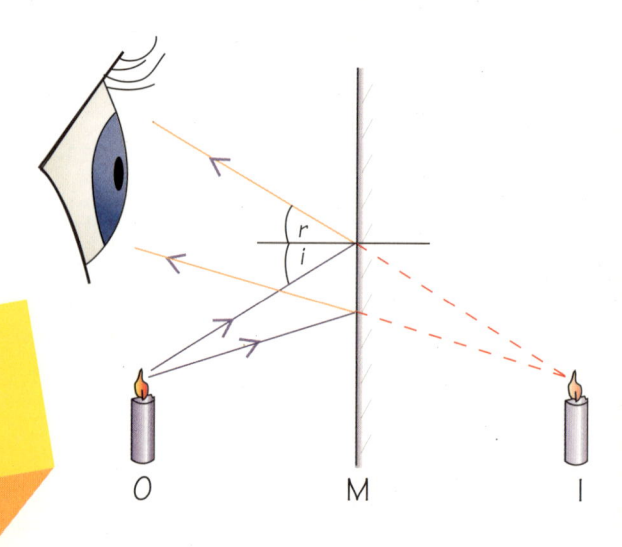

Refraction

- **Less dense to more dense** – direction changes.
- **Direction at A** – towards normal.
- **Direction at B** – away from normal.
- **Denser medium** – greater refraction.
- **Refractive index** – measure of refraction
  - sin i / sin r
  - about 1.5 for glass.
- **Example** – bottom of swimming pool appears nearer.

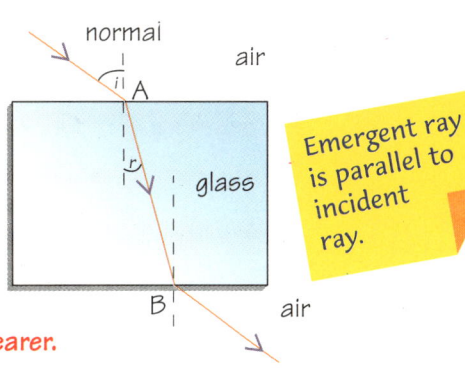

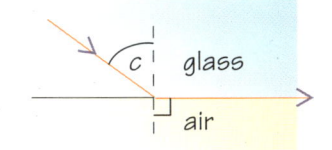

Emergent ray is parallel to incident ray.

- **Critical angle** c – light refracted at 90°.
- **Incident angle greater** – all light reflected back.
- This is called **total internal reflection** (TIR).
- **Examples** – optical fibre
  - prism binoculars.

Note that this only occurs moving from more dense to less dense.

Diffraction

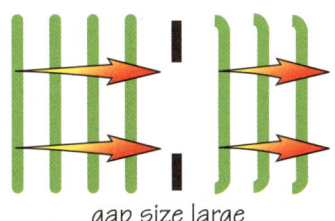

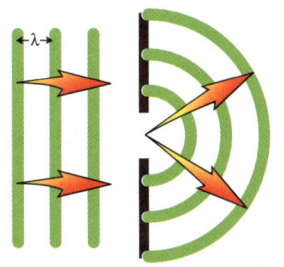

gap size large

gap same size as wavelength

- **Waves spread out** – past obstacle/through gap.
- **Gap size** – about same as wavelength.
- **Examples** – sound heard around corners
  - radio signals received in shadow of hills.

Electromagnetic spectrum

wavelength decreases →   ← frequency decreases

A mnemonic such as Reading Is Lousy Unless Extremely Good will help you to remember the order.

	Radio	Infra-red	Light	Ultra-violet	X-rays	Gamma-rays
Source	Vibrating electrons	Sun Hot bodies	Sun Luminous objects	Sun Mercury Vapour lamp	Stars X-ray tube	Radioactive substances
Detector	Radio aerial	Skin IR photographic film	Eye Photographic film	Skin (tanning) Photographic film	Photographic film	GM tube Photographic film
Use	Communication Cooking (microwaves)	Heating Remote control	Seeing Photography Photosynthesis	Security marking Fluorescent lamps	Medical photographs Astronomy	Cancer treatment

- **Family of waves.**
- **Speed** – same = 3×10^8 m/s.
- **Different wavelengths** – reflected, refracted, etc. differently.

PHYSICAL PROCESSES

Radio waves

- **Transmit** – radio/TV over Earth's surface.
- **Longer wavelength** – **reflected** from ionosphere (electrically charged layer in upper atmosphere)
  – enables communication despite curvature of Earth's surface.
- **Shorter wavelength** – can penetrate ionosphere
  – used for communication with satellites
  – water molecules can strongly absorb one particular frequency, so used for cooking.

Infra-red

- **Readily absorbed** – by rough, **black** surfaces.
- **Strongly reflected** – by polished, **light** surfaces.
- Uses – grills, toasters, radiant heaters, optical fibre communication, remote control of TV/VCR.

Light

- **Used in optical fibres** – medical endoscopes to see inside patient's body.
- **White light** – split into **colours** by prism.
- **Spectrum** – **colour depends on wavelength.**
- **Most refracted** – **violet.**
- **Least refracted** – **red.**
- **Brightness** – **depends on intensity/amplitude** of wave.
- **Colour filters** – **absorb** different **wavelengths** (colour subtraction).
- **Coloured objects** – behave **like** colour **filters.**

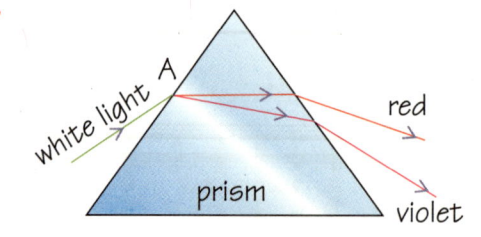

> **Examiner's tip**
> Students often do not show the red and violet rays spreading out from point A.

Ultra-violet

- **Uses** – sunbeds/fluorescent lamps/security coding where special coating absorbs radiation and emits light.

X-radiation

- **Does not easily pass through bone/metal.**
- **Used to produce shadow pictures** of people/materials.

Gamma radiation

- **Kills harmful bacteria** in food.
- **Sterilises** surgical instruments.
- **Kills cancer cells.**

Effect on living cells

- **Microwaves** – absorbed by water in cells
  – cells may be damaged/killed by heat released.
- **Infra-red** – absorbed by skin
  – felt as heat.
- **Ultra-violet** – can pass through skin to deep tissue
  – darker skin absorbs more so less reaches deep tissue.
- **X-rays/Gamma rays** – pass through soft tissue
  – some absorbed by cells.

> **Examiner's tip**
> Note that microwaves, infra-red and ultra-violet can all cause heating effects.

Using light

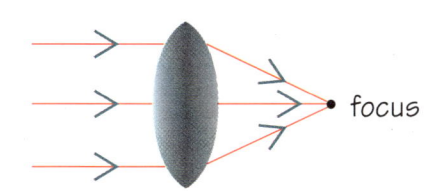

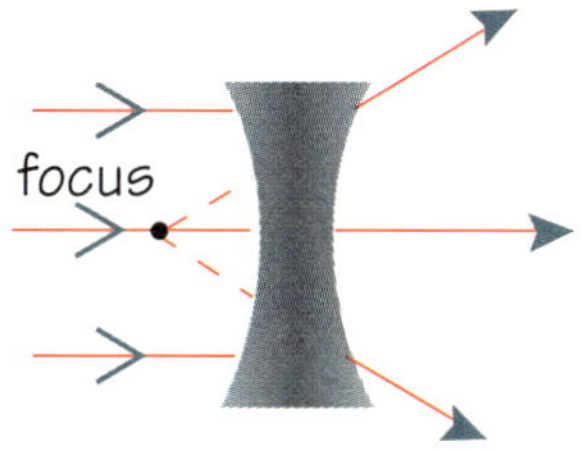

1 Convex lens
- **focus** – real; parallel light converges
- **real image** formed
- **examples** – eye, camera, magnifier.

2 Concave lens
- **focus** – virtual; light spreads out
- **virtual image formed**
- **example** – spectacle lens (short sight).

3 Eye
- **cornea/lens** – focus light
- **image** – inverted/smaller
- **thicker lens** – converges light more
- **far objects** – lens thinner.

- **perfect eye** – light focused on retina
- **ciliary muscles** – control lens shape
- **retina** – lens thicker
- **near objects** – light-sensitive layer.

Eye defects
- **Clouded cornea** – replace with clear plastic.
- **Short sight** – eye too long/lens too thick
  – correct with concave lens.
- **Long sight** – eye too short/lens too thin
  – correct with convex lens.

> The eye is similar in many ways to a simple camera.

short sight   long sight

correction   correction

> **Examiner's tip**
> Questions are often set on eye defects.

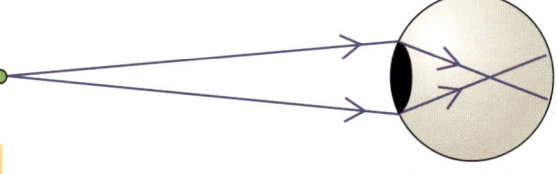

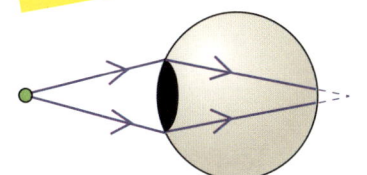

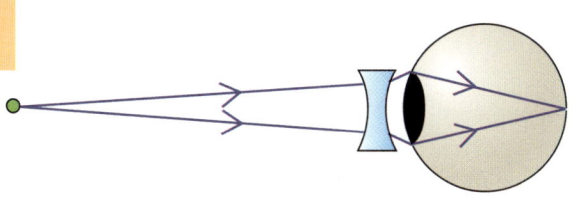

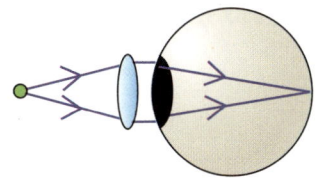

Sound

- **Vibration produces sound.**
- **Examples** – guitar string, drum skin, whistle.
- **Volume** – depends on amplitude.
- **Pitch** – depends on frequency.
- **Speed** – in air about 340 m/s
  – faster in denser substances, e.g. water
  – measure by timing echoes.

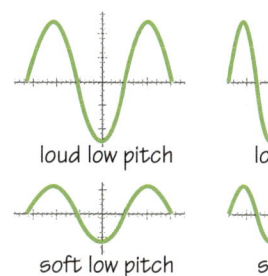

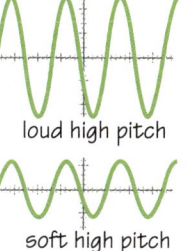

loud low pitch   loud high pitch
soft low pitch   soft high pitch

> These are patterns seen on an oscilloscope. These represent pure notes; everyday sounds are not usually so smooth.

PHYSICAL PROCESSES

Using sound

1 Ear
- Hearing range – up to 20 kHz in humans
  - dogs hear sounds above 20 kHz
  - limit decreases with age
  - human hearing is very sensitive to frequencies of around 3 kHz.
- Ear drum – vibrates.
- Middle ear – bones vibrate.
- Inner ear – liquid in cochlea vibrates.
- Noise pollution – can damage hearing
  - caused by very loud sounds.

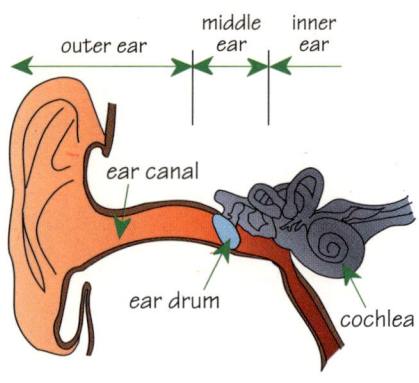

2 Ultrasound
- Definition – above 20 kHz.
- Reflection – at boundary between media
  - time for detection gives distance.
- Bats – detect objects from echoes.
- Sea – measure depth
  - detect fish shoals.
- Industry – cleaning delicate objects
  - detect flaws in metal casings.
- Hospital – pre-natal scanning.

Examiner's tip
Ultrasonic scanning is thought to be safer than using X-rays; state this as a main advantage in an answer.

3 Seismic waves – earthquakes
- P waves – longitudinal
  - fast
  - travel through solids, liquids.
- S waves – transverse
  - slower
  - only travel through solids.
- Refraction – at boundary between media
  - indicates changing density.

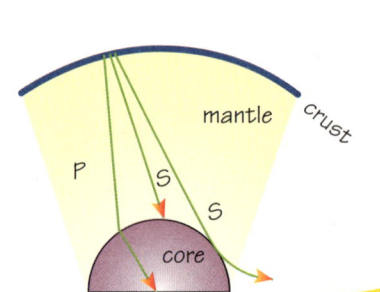

P comes **before** S in the alphabet, so P waves arrive **before** S waves.

Observations suggest Earth – made of layers
- has thin crust
- has solid mantle with density increasing with depth
- has core just over half Earth diameter
- has core with liquid outer and solid inner part.

S-waves cannot pass through liquid core.

Questions

1. Here is a waveform that you may see on an oscilloscope screen.

    (a) Measure i) its wavelength _____ cm

    ii) its amplitude _____ cm

    (b) It takes 0.01 s for this waveform to travel across the screen.

    Calculate i) its frequency _____

    _____

    ii) its speed _____

    _____

2. (a) Copy and complete the diagram to show how an image is formed in a plane mirror.

    (b) Is the image 'real' or 'virtual'? Explain your answer. _____

    _____

3. Echo location techniques can be used by a fishing trawler to find shoals of fish in the sea.

    (a) Describe how this works. _____

    _____

    (b) If the speed of sound in water is 1550 m/s and it takes 0.3 s for an echo to be received, how deep is the shoal? _____

    _____

4. Name two differences between P and S waves sent out from the epicentre of an earthquake.

    i) _____

    ii) _____

PHYSICAL PROCESSES

PHYSICAL PROCESSES

The Earth and beyond

The Solar System

Satellites

- **Moon** – natural satellite.
- **Sputnik** – example of artificial satellite – USSR 1957.
- **Use** – beam information to places on Earth a long way apart, e.g. TV
  - monitor conditions etc. on Earth, e.g. weather
  - acts as observatory since no interference from atmosphere.
- **Orbits** – communication satellite uses high equatorial orbit; scans same point continuously
  - monitoring satellite uses low polar orbit; scans whole N or S hemisphere each day.

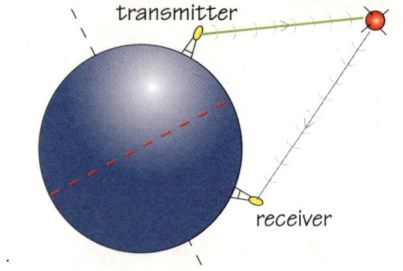

Examiner's tip: There may well be a question on uses of satellites.

Orbit of communication satellite is 'geostationary'. Speed of rotation same as Earth.

Gravity

- **Attraction** – all bodies in Universe.
- **Gravitational force (g) greater if**
  - mass of bodies greater
  - distance apart less; 2 × distance = $\frac{1}{4}$ of force.
- **Earth** – g = 10 N/kg.
- **Larger planets**, e.g. Jupiter – g greater.
- **Smaller planets**, e.g. Mercury – g smaller.
- **Weightlessness** – no weight
  - orbiting satellite
  - far out in space.

An apple weigh about 1 Newton!

Orbital motion

- **Planetary orbits** – elliptical not circular.
- **Comets** – orbit very elliptical
  - much closer to Sun at times → visible.
- **Orbit larger** – further from Sun
  - longer time for orbit.
- **Small bodies**, e.g. satellites – need certain speed to stay in orbit.
- **Asteroids** – group of rock debris between Mars and Jupiter.

Note that the orbit of Pluto is at an angle to those of the other planets.

You should know the order of the planets - My Very Easy Method Just Speeds Up Naming Planets will help you!

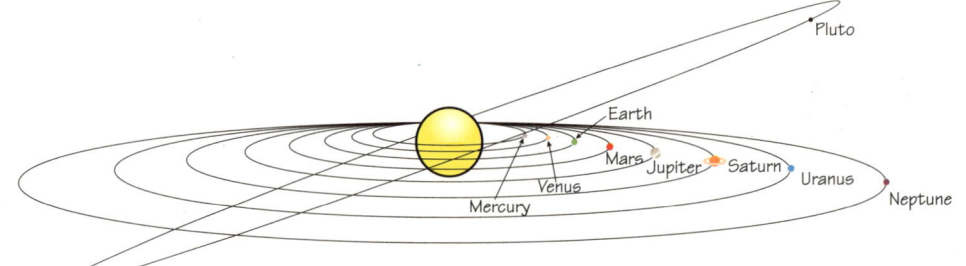

Solar System (not to scale)

- **Earth** – tilt of axis to plane of orbit explains seasonal changes, length of daylight
  - spin on axis explains day and night, apparent motion of stars.

Universe

Stars

- **Sun** – one of millions of stars.
- **Galaxy** – group of stars
    - stars millions of times further apart than planets from Sun.
- **Universe** – at least one thousand million (billion) galaxies
    - galaxies millions of times further apart than stars.

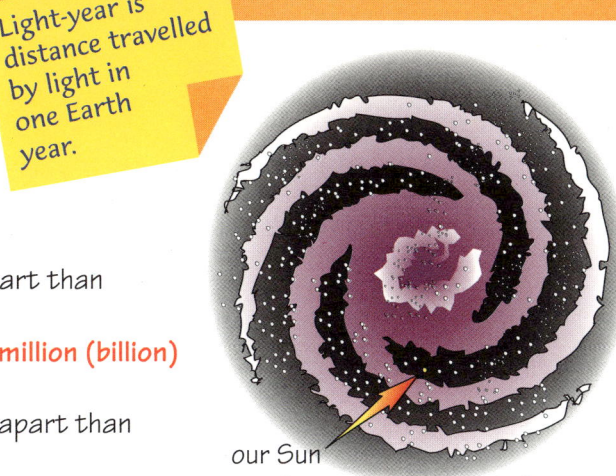

> Light-year is distance travelled by light in one Earth year.

our Sun
Our galaxy (Milky Way) would look like this from space

Life of a star

- **Birth** – dust + gas $\xrightarrow{\text{immense gravity}}$ star.
- **Mass** – very large compared to planets.
- **Volume** – Sun (small star) million times larger volume than Earth.
- **Density** – star matter millions of times denser than Earth matter.
- **Heat** – stars are balls of very hot gases
    - creates forces tending to expansion of star
    - forces balance → stability (e.g. our Sun).
- **Size change** – stable for millions of years
    - expansion → red giant → rapid contraction → supernova explosion
        ↓   ↓
    contraction   neutron star (very dense)
        ↓   ↓
    white dwarf (very small, cold)   black hole (no light escapes)

Examiner's tip
Make sure your answers contain only the key important points.

Energy production in a star

- **Light nuclei** – fuse → heavier nuclei
    - vast energy release
    - present in Sun/inner planets → solar system formed from explosions of old stars.

Examiner's tip
Nuclear fusion is not the same process as nuclear fission (which occurs in nuclear power stations).

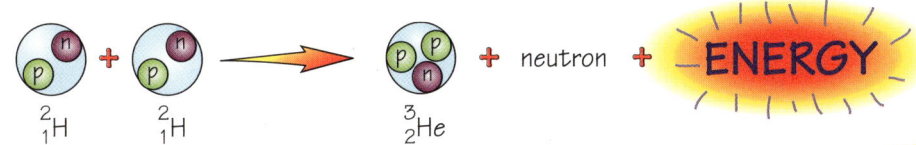

$^{2}_{1}H$ + $^{2}_{1}H$ → $^{3}_{2}He$ + neutron + ENERGY

heavy hydrogen (deuterium)   helium nucleus

Universe

- **Red shift** – light from other galaxies shifted to red end of spectrum.
- **More red shift** – galaxies further away → galaxies receding fast → universe expanding.
- **Big Bang** – theory on possible start of universe
    - uses red shift observations
    - universe began from explosion of matter.
- **Age** – at least 15 billion years old.

> Some scientists believe that the Universe has always existed – this is called the Steady State theory.

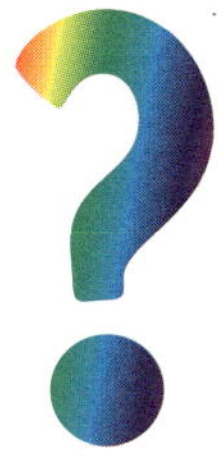

PHYSICAL PROCESSES

85

Questions

1. One use of artificial satellites is to broadcast information around the world.

    (a) What is the name we give to this type of satellite?
    _____

    (b) Name and describe the use of one other type of satellite.
    _____

2. Astronauts in an orbiting spacecraft experience weightlessness.

    (a) What does this mean?
    _____

    (b) The spacecraft is still within the gravitational field of the Earth. Explain why the astronauts are weightless.
    _____
    _____

3. Halley's comet is seen in the sky every 75 years.

    (a) With the aid of a diagram explain why it is seen only periodically and not all the time.

    (b) On your diagram draw the path of a second comet that would only ever be seen once from the Earth.

4. Describe the stages in the evolution of a star resulting in the formation of a neutron star.
    _____
    _____
    _____
    _____
    _____

Energy resources and energy transfer

Thermal energy

- Thermal energy – transferred from hot to cold body.

Conduction

- Adjacent particles transfer energy.
- Metal – good conductor
  - hotter → more kinetic energy (KE) for free electrons → diffusion
  - also energy transfer by collision.
- Non-metals/liquids – poor conductors.
- Gases – very poor conductors.

Note that evaporation also causes heat loss.

Convection

- Gas/liquid – particles gain KE → expansion
  - hotter parts less dense → rise up
  - colder parts more dense → replace hotter parts.
- Examples – hot air balloon, sea breeze.

Radiation

- Energy transfer by waves.
- Part of electromagnetic spectrum (infra-red, IR).
- Emission – hot bodies
  - dark, matt surfaces.

Most heat loss from a building is via the roof.

Examiner's tip
You should know about sources of heat loss from e.g. home, cup of tea + ways of reducing the loss by insulation.

Energy efficiency

$$\text{Efficiency} = \frac{\text{useful energy transferred}}{\text{total energy supplied}}$$

- Unuseful energy – wasted
  - reduces efficiency.
- Energy supplied – heats surroundings
  - increasingly spread out
  - more difficult to use for energy transfer.

Energy resources

- Renewable – will not run out, e.g. wood, tides, wind.
- Non-renewable – cannot be replaced, e.g. fossil fuels, nuclear.
- Power station – generates electricity from both types.
- Steam – produced by non-renewable resources + wood/geothermal
  - drives turbines.
- Turbines – driven directly by renewable resources
  - solar cells produce electricity directly
  - turn generators → electricity.

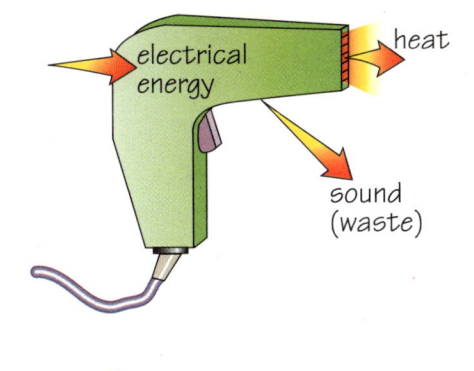

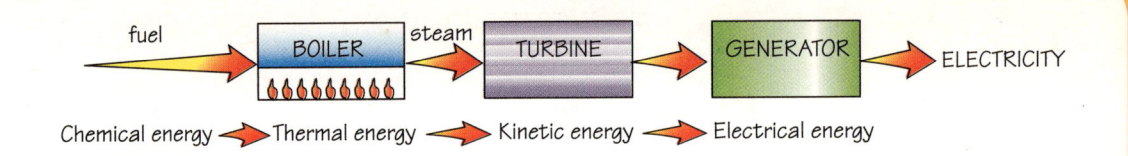

fuel → BOILER → steam → TURBINE → GENERATOR → ELECTRICITY

Chemical energy → Thermal energy → Kinetic energy → Electrical energy

Non-renewable vs Renewable

- Will run out
- waste
- fuel costs
- transportation costs high
- building costs high.

- Will not run out
- no waste
- no fuel costs
- no transportation costs
- generating equipment costs high.
  (Note: above excludes wood.)

Work

Work done = force x distance
= energy transferred

- Units – joules (J).
- 1 J – 1 Nm.

Power = work done / time taken
= rate of energy transfer

- Units – watts (W).
- 1 W – 1 J/s.

A ramp is a machine. Machines make work easier. Other examples include: spanner, pulley, lever.

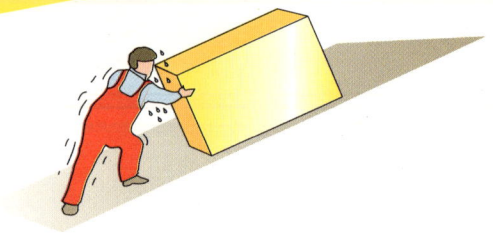

Kinetic energy (KE)

- Moving object has KE.
- KE depends on mass and speed.

$$KE = 1/2 \times mass \times (speed)^2$$

- Units – J.
- Example – moving car.

Examiner's tip
Students often forget that speed must be squared.

A high diver exchanges her PE for KE on the way down.

Potential energy (PE)

- Gravitational PE – energy stored
  – depends on weight + height
  – example: walking upstairs.

Gravitational PE = weight x change in vertical height

- Units – J.
- Weight depends on – mass
  – gravitational field strength, g.

Weight = mass x g

- Gravitational field strength – on Earth about 10 N/kg.
  – on Moon about 1.7 N/kg.
- Elastic PE – energy stored
  – depends on change in shape of body
  – examples: stretched spring, catapult.

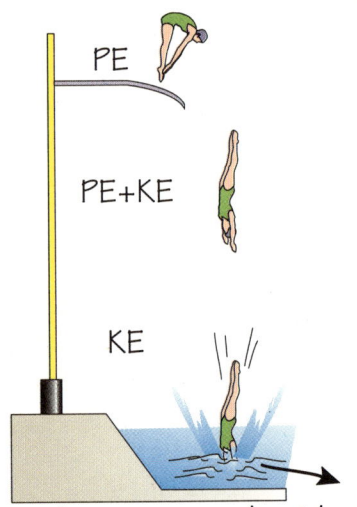

PE
PE+KE
KE
heat/sound

Questions

1. A 'radiator' used in home central heating should really be called a 'convector'. Do you agree? Explain your answer.

   _____
   _____

2. An electric kettle is rated at 1 kW.

   It takes 30 s to heat up a certain mass of water.

   (a) If 1 W = 1 J/s, how much energy is supplied to the kettle?

   _____

   (b) 10 kJ of energy is wasted. Calculate the efficiency of the kettle.

   _____

   (c) i) How is this energy wasted? _____

       ii) How could this waste be reduced? _____

3. (a) Name a renewable energy resource. _____

   (b) Describe three main advantages that renewable energy resources have over non-renewable resources for the generation of electricity.

   i) _____
   ii) _____
   iii) _____

4. Julie runs up a staircase. Each step is 20 cm high. There are 10 steps to the top. If her weight is 450 N,

   (a) how much work must she do to reach the top?

   _____
   _____
   _____

   20 cm

   (b) what power does she develop if it takes her 3 s?

   _____
   _____
   _____

PHYSICAL PROCESSES

Radioactivity

Atomic structure

- **Atoms** – tiny central nucleus with electrons outside.
- **Radioactivity** – emitted when nucleus changes.
- **Nucleus** – protons (p) + neutrons (n).
- **Electrons** (e) – orbit around nucleus.
- **Plum pudding model** – plums (electrons) embedded in atom.
- **Alpha scattering** → nucleus has positive (+) charge.

	Mass	Charge
p	1	+1
n	1	0
e	negligible	−1

Number of p = number of e overall charge on atom is zero..

Elements

- **Proton number** – same for atoms of same element.
- **Nucleon (mass) number** – total number of p + n.
- **Isotope** – atoms of same element with different number of n.
- **Radioactive isotope** – isotopes with unstable nuclei
  – also known as **radioisotope** or **radionuclide**.
- **Disintegration** – nuclei break up → number of n and p may change → different element if p changes.
- **Radiation emission** – continually
  – random.

e.g. $^{4}_{2}He$

nucleon number — A
element symbol
proton number — Z

Nucleon number minus proton number gives number of neutrons.

Note that g decay has no effect on nucleon or proton number.

Types of radiation

Type	Symbol	Stopped by	Composition	Charge	Mass
alpha	α	thin sheet of paper	2p + 2n (He nucleus)	+	large
beta	β	2 mm metal	electrons; n → p + e	−	tiny
gamma	γ	reduced by thick concrete/lead	Em radiation (very high frequency)	0	0

Look at composition to predict new proton and nucleon numbers.

Sources of radiation

- **Space** – cosmic rays.
- **Ground/building materials.**
- **Food.**
- **Medical** – radiography, e.g. chest X-ray
  – treatment, e.g. cancer.
- **Nuclear power station.**

Radiation is a natural part of our environment; it is called 'background radiation'.

Dangers of radiation

- **Absorption** by material → **ionisation** of atoms.
- **Cell damage** – **may kill/cause cancer**
  - alpha source most dangerous in body
  - beta, gamma sources most dangerous outside body.

Uses of radiation

- **Monitor/control thickness** – greater absorption by thicker material
  - alpha and beta.
- **Medical treatment** – kill cancer cells
  - gamma.
- **Tracers** – trace path of fluids
  - medicine, agriculture.

> GM tube measures activity.

Half-life

- **Radioactive atoms** → **radiation** → **stable** (non-radioactive atoms).
- **Activity decreases with time.**
- **Half-life** – **time** for activity/count rate **to halve**
  - different for different radioisotopes, e.g. Na–24 is 15 hours, Pt–239 is 24000 years.
- **Carbon dating** – half-life 5730 years
  - used to find **age of once living radioactive material**.

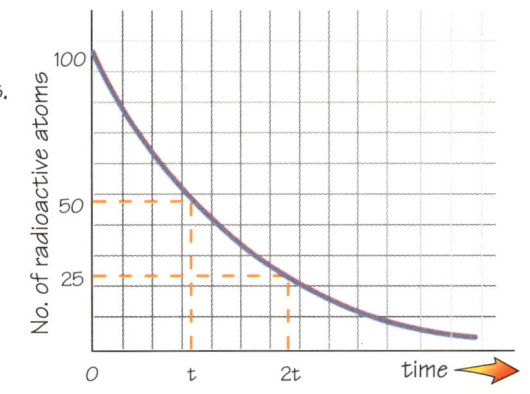

> **Examiner's tip**
> In practice, background count should be subtracted.

> The graph shows the decay of a radionuclide. Half-life = t.

Nuclear fission

- **Neutrons** – fired at large nucleus.
- **Nucleus splits** → neutrons released → **chain reaction**.
- **New atoms also radioactive.**
- **Energy released** – **much larger than** associated with a **chemical bond**.
- **Nuclear power stations release energy by nuclear fission.**
- **Sun releases energy by nuclear fusion.**

> In a nuclear power station, the chain reaction is slowed/stopped by control rods; they absorb the neutrons.

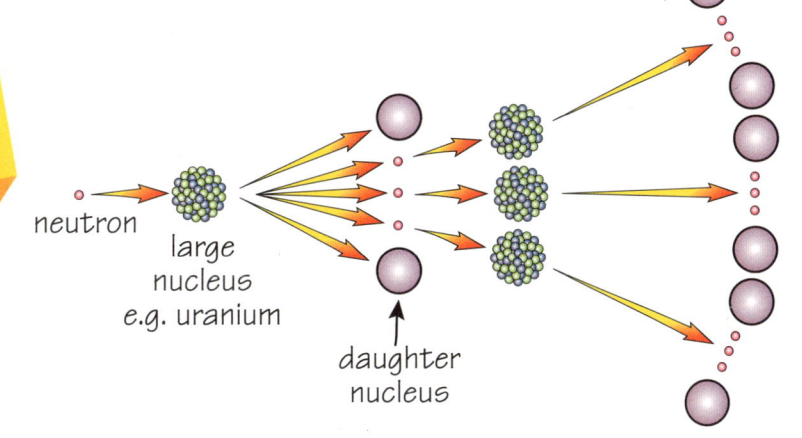

neutron → large nucleus e.g. uranium → daughter nucleus

Questions

1 (a) Explain the 'plum pudding' model of the atom.

_____

_____

(b) How was this model modified from the alpha scattering experiments?

_____

_____

2 Name two ways in which gamma radiation differs from either alpha or beta radiation.

(a) _____

(b) _____

3 The activity of a sample of a radionuclide was measured. It was found to be 3000 counts/min at 9 am. By 11 am this had decreased to 750 counts/min.

(a) What instrument is used to measure the activity? _____

(b) Calculate the half-life of the sample.

_____

_____

_____

(c) When the detector was moved away, the experimenter noticed that it still recorded a low count rate. Why?

_____

_____

4 Steel sheets are produced in a steel mill. The sheets are rolled out to a certain thickness as they pass along a conveyor belt. By drawing a diagram, explain how a radioactive source can be used to monitor and control the thickness.

Answers

Electricity and magnetism

1 Negative charges on rod – transfer to cloth – makes cloth –ve and rod +ve
2 (a) 6 V (b) Current through each lamp = 1.5 A, R = V/I = 6/1.5 = 4Ω
3 (a) I = P/V = 1500/250 = 6 A Use 10 A fuse (b) 7 days @ 1/3 hour per day = 7/3 hours. Cost = 1.5 x 7/3 x 6p = 21 p
4 (a) Output voltage bigger than input voltage (b) Number of turns needed = 7.0/2.0 x 100 = 350

Forces and motion

1 (a) Constant acceleration (b) i) Acceleration = 6/30 = 0.2 m/s^2 ii) Distance = area under graph = area of triangle = ½ x 30 x 6 = 90 m
2 (a) Resultant force = 6500 – 850 = 5650 N. Acceleration = F/m = 5650/1200 = 4.71 m/s^2 (b) Reaction time, weather, condition of tyres/brakes/road
3 { moment = 120 x 0.5 = 60 Nm; [moment = W x 1.25 = 1.25W Nm
To balance, 1.25 W = 60, W = 48 N
4 Momentum before collision = 5000 x 10 + 3000 x 5 = 50 000 + 15 000 = 65 000 kgm/s; Momentum after collision = 8000 x v kgm/s
Conservation of momentum → 8000 v = 65 000; v = 8.13 m/s
5 Force = 0.4/0.1 x 150 = 4 x 150 = 600 N

Waves

1 (a) i) Wavelength = 2.75 cm ii) Amplitude = 0.75 cm (b) i) 11 ½ wavelengths fit on screen in 0.01 s; so, period = 0.02/3, ∴ frequency = 3/0.02 = 150 Hz
ii) Speed = 150 x 2.5 = 412.5 m/s
2 (a)

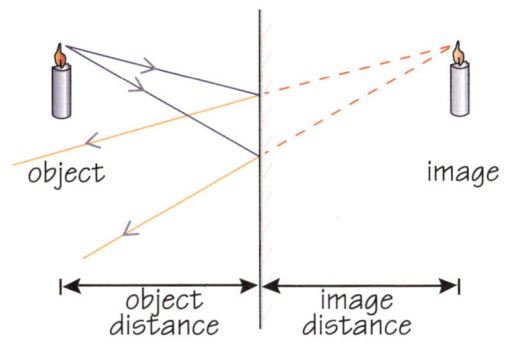

(b) Virtual. Not really there/cannot be projected on a screen.
3 (a) (Ultrasonic) pulse sent into water. Time to return to receiver measured. Depth of shoal = speed x time (b) 0.3 s for signal to travel there and back. Use time = 0.15 s; Depth = 1550 x 0.15 = 232.5 m
4 P – longitudinal, fast, travel through solids + liquids; S – transverse, slow, travel only through solids

The Earth and beyond

1 (a) Communications satellite **(b)** Monitoring – gather Earth data on e.g. weather; observatory – gather space data on e.g. planets **2 (a)** No weight. **(b)** Spacecraft pulled towards Earth by gravitational force; astronauts pulled towards spacecraft; floor falls away as fast as astronauts fall toward floor; no contact with floor; therefore zero weight
3 (a) Long elliptical orbit only visible when near Earth **(b)** Parabolic path – never returns.
4 Dust + gas → star born → stability → expansion → red giant → rapid contraction → supernova → neutron star

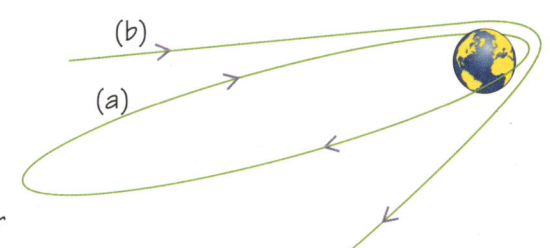

Energy resources and energy transfer

1 Yes – little radiated heat – room mainly heated by creation of convection current
2 (a) 1kW = 1000 W; Energy supplied = 1000 × 30 s = 30000 J = 30 kJ
(b) Efficiency = 20 kJ/30kJ × 100 = 66.7 % **(c)** i) Heats up kettle body/surroundings; sound energy produced ii) Insulate kettle e.g. wrap insulation around
3 (a) Any of wind, wave, tidal, geothermal, solar, wood **(b)** Will not run out, no waste, no fuel cost, no transportation cost
4 (a) Work = force × distance = 450 × 10 × 0.2 = 900 J **(b)** Power = work done/time taken = 900/3 = 300 W

Radioactivity

1 (a) Plums = electrons, electrons embedded in atom **(b)** Atom has central nucleus; nucleus tiny; nucleus + ve; electrons orbit nucleus; most of atom empty space
2 Gamma – wave not particle – no mass/charge – travels at speed of light/ 3×10^8 m/s
3 (a) GM tube/counter **(b)** 9am – 3000 counts/min; 11am – 750 counts/min; therefore 2 hours → drops to ¼; 1 hour → drops to ½; half-life = 1 hour
(c) Recording background radiation
4 Radioactive source; source above/below sheets; detector below/above sheets; correct thickness → p counts/min recorded; thickness too big → less than p recorded; thickness too small → more than p recorded; link detector via feedback to motor; motor controls roller pressure

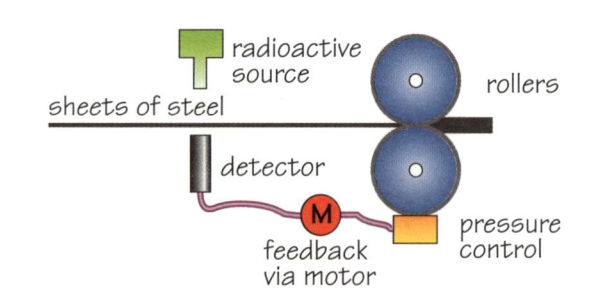

Index

acceleration 74
acids 53–4, 56–7
air
   chemical products 48–51
alcohol 14, 55–7
alkali 53–4, 57
alkali metals 41
aluminium 46, 61
ammonia 48–50, 62
assimilation in plants 17
atmosphere 65–6
atomic structure 36–7, 90
blood 9
   circulation and vessels 8–9
   sugar 11–12
bond energy 63–4
bonding 37–9
Boyle's law 76
carbon cycle 33, 66
catalysts 61–2
cell division 22–3
cells 4–5
chemical equations 60–1
circular motion 76
cloning 25
competition between organisms 28
contact process 51–3, 62
copper 47, 52–3
crude oil 66–7
diet and digestion 7–8
diffraction 79
diseases 14
   inherited 23–4
DNA 24
drugs 14
ear 82
Earth 65, 82, 84
earthquakes 82
electricity 70–2, 88
electrolysis 45–7, 70
electromagnetic spectrum 79–80
electromagnetism 72
electron arrangements 36–9
electrostatics 70
elements 90
energy 87–9
   chemical reactions 63–4
   production in stars 85
   sources for organisms 30–1

environmental effects of man 28–9
enzymes 62
equations 60–1
equilibria 48–51, 62
evolution 26
extraction 44–6
eye 11, 78, 81
fertilisers 29, 49–51
fertility 12
food chains and pyramids 31
food production 30
forces 74–6, 88
fossils 26
fractional distillation 66–7
free fall 75
friction 75
genetic engineering 25
genetics 22–6
geology 64–5
gravity 19, 76, 84, 88
Haber process 48–9, 62
half-life 91
halogens 41–2
heart 8
homeostasis 12–13
hormones 11–12, 19
hydrocarbons 66–7
indicators 54
iron 39, 44–5, 54–5, 61
kidneys 13
kinetic energy 88
Le Chatelier's principle 48–9, 62
life characteristics 4
liver 7, 9, 11–13
lungs 9–10, 12
macromolecules 67
magnetism 72
mass 76, 88
menstrual cycle 12
metals 38–9, 41–2, 44–7, 52–5, 61
   extraction from ores 44–7
microbes 14, 31–2
minerals 18
moles 60–1
momentum 76
mutations 24–5
nervous system 10–11
nitrogen cycle 33
noble gases 42
nuclear fission 91
nuclear fusion 85

nutrients 7, 18, 30–1
orbits 84
organs 5
osmosis 20
periodic table 41
petroleum 66–7
pH 54
photosynthesis 16–17
plants 16–20
pollution 28, 31, 51
population 28
potential energy 88
power 88
pressure 49, 61, 76
protein synthesis 24
radiation 80, 90–1
radioactivity 90–1
reaction rates 61–4
reflection 78
refraction 79–80
respiration 9–10
rocks 64–5
rusting 54–5
salts 52–3, 55–9
satellites 84
selection of organisms 26
solubility 57
sound 81–2
speed 74, 76, 88
stars 85
states of matter 36
steel 39, 45
stopping distances 75
sulphuric acid 51–3, 55–6, 62
systems in biology 5
temperature control 13
thermal energy 87
tissue culture 25
tissues 5
titration 52
transformers 72
transition metals 41–2
transpiration 20
universe 85
variation between organisms 22
velocity 74, 76, 88
water 13, 20, 58–9
waves 78–82
weight 74, 88
work 88

Success or your money back

Letts' market leading series GCSE Revision Notes gives you everything you need for exam success. We're so confident that they're the best revision books you can buy that if you don't make the grade we will give you your money back!

HERE'S HOW IT WORKS
Register the Letts GCSE Revision Notes you buy by writing to us within 28 days of purchase with the following information:
- Name
- Address
- Postcode
- Subject of GCSE Revision Notes book bought – please include your till receipt or school name and address and subject teacher
- Probable tier you will enter

To make a **claim**, compare your results to the grades below. If any of your grades qualify for a refund, make a claim by writing to us within 28 days of getting your results, enclosing a copy of your original exam slip. If you do not register, you won't be able to make a claim after you receive your results.

CLAIM IF…
You're a Higher Tier student and get a grade D or below
You're an Intermediate Tier student and get a grade E or below
You're a Foundation Tier student and get a grade F or below
You're a Scottish Standard Grade Student taking Credit and General Level exams and get a grade 4 or below
This offer is not open to Scottish Standard Grade students sitting Foundation Level exams.

Registration and claim address:
Letts Success or Your Money Back Offer, Letts Educational, Aldine Place, London W12 8AW

TERMS AND CONDITIONS
1. Applies to the Letts GCSE Revision Notes series only
2. Registration of purchases must be received by Letts Educational within 28 days of the purchase date
3. Registration must be accompanied by a valid till receipt
4. All money back claims must be received by Letts Educational within 28 days of receiving exam results
5. All claims must be accompanied by a letter stating the claim and a copy of the relevant exam results slip
6. Claims will be invalid if they do not match with the original registered subjects
7. Letts Educational reserves the right to seek confirmation of the level of entry of the claimant
8. Responsibility cannot be accepted for lost, delayed or damaged applications, or applications received outside of the stated registration / claim timescales
9. Proof of posting will not be accepted as proof of delivery
10. Offer only available to GCSE students studying within the UK
11. SUCCESS OR YOUR MONEY BACK is promoted by Letts Educational, Aldine Place, London W12 8AW
12. Registration indicates a complete acceptance of these rules
13. Illegible entries will be disqualified
14. In all matters, the decision of Letts Educational will be final and no correspondence will be entered into

Letts Educational
Aldine Place
London W12 8AW
Tel: 020 8740 2266
Fax: 020 8743 8451
email: mail@lettsed.co.uk
website: www.letts-education.com

Every effort has been made to trace copyright holders and obtain their permission for the use of copyright material. The authors and publishers will gladly receive information enabling them to rectify any error or omission in subsequent editions.

First published 1998
Reprinted 1998, 1999
New edition 1999
This edition 2000

Text © John Dobson, Paul Levy, Nick Parmar 2000
Editorial and design by Hart McLeod, Cambridge

All our Rights Reserved. No part of this publication may be reproduced, stored in a retrieval system, or transmitted, in any form or by any means, electronic, mechanical, photocopying, recording or otherwise, without the prior permission of Letts Educational.

British Library Cataloguing in Publication Data
A CIP record for this book is available from the British Library.

ISBN 1 84085 470 7

Printed in Italy

Letts Educational Limited is a division of Granada Learning Limited, part of the Granada Media Group.